CENTRAL PLANNING
A Case Study of China

About the Author

K.L. Datta, an officer of the Indian Economic Service, is presently the Advisor, Directorate of Development Planning, Ministry of National Economy, Sultanate of Oman. He has worked in different capacities in the Planning Commission of India and also as Deputy Secretary in the Ministry of Finance, Government of India. He did his M.A. (Economics) from Calcutta University as well as from Manchester University. He has to his credit a book *Facets of Indian Poverty*, published by Concept Publishing Company (2002)

CENTRAL PLANNING
A Case Study of China

K.L. DATTA

CONCEPT PUBLISHING COMPANY, NEW DELHI-110059

ISBN 81-8069-061-X

First Published 2004

Published and Printed by
Ashok Kumar Mittal
Concept Publishing Company
A/15-16, Commercial Block, Mohan Garden
New Delhi-110059 (INDIA)

Phones : 25351460, 25351794
Fax : 091-11-25357103
Email : publishing@conceptpub.com.

To My Parents

Foreword

The study focuses on the strategy of economic development in China under the aegis of central planning and its outcome. K. L. Datta, who has done it is eminently qualified to do so. He has both the expert theoretical background and vast experience in the Perspective Planning Division of the Indian Planning Commission, to conduct the study.

Datta relies on official statistics of China, but his deep insights into the techniques of mining data, gives him a perspective, which is missed out by most superficial commentators. Datta it may be recalled was one of the principal scientific workers in the Task Force which defined India's poverty line, which still endures, although the work was done under my overall supervision in the Seventies. He is able, therefore, to question the definitional tautologies on everything is alright in China.

On attaining liberation in October 1949 after a prolonged armed struggle, a disjoint and fragmented economy was consolidated by 1952. The transport and communication network, which was severely disrupted during the civil war, was restored. Runaway inflation was brought under control. China entered into an era of planned economic development in 1953 with the launching of its First Five Year Plan. It's tryst with central planning ended in the Third Plenary Session of the Eleventh Central Committee of the Chinese Communist Party held in December 1978.

The dismantling of the central planning apparatus began in 1979 with the introduction of the policies of economic reform and liberalization replacing the different agents of the government as decision makers. The state began to withdraw from economic sectors allowing space to the private sector and took upon itself the responsibility of creating a suitable environment for growth and development instead of directly participating in production and distribution. The implementation of policies of economic reform and liberalization in China during the past two decades has been watched with interest both within and outside the country. The last chapter outlines the course of reforms and also serves as a comparison between central planning and the market-led development in China.

Datta dispels the myth that China was a closed economy - describes the planning structure of the country – the adoption of Russian model and its rejection. The Great Leap Forward is described in detail as it was politics with slogans from economics and created havoc on the lives of millions of people. The emphasis on industry – mainly to demonstrate that high industrial growth failed to improve the quality of life of the people. China's total product, Datta notes, is equivalent to India's gross value of output, but national income is not equivalent to value added. The consequences of misdirected investment are discussed in some detail.

The rate of growth of income and consumption in the central plan era (1952-78) was modest. Considerable inter-regional and inter-personal inequality in the distribution of income and consumption accompanied this modest rate of economic growth. However, the inequality in per capita income was more than that in per capita consumption, which, in turn, was more than that in per capita foodgrain consumption.

Datta brings out that the economy gathered considerable momentum during the initial period of restoration following the liberation. The tables turned from 1958 with the Great Leap Forward, and the birth of the commune organization. The major macro-economic variables began to stagnate from as early as 1961.

Land reform is discussed in detail since it was a revolution effected by the peasants. The political slogan was: encircle the cities by villages – a strategy distinctly different form that adopted in the Russian (Bolshevik) Revolution in which the industrial workers played the dominant role. Land reform carried out immediately after revolution (by enacting the Agrarian reforms Law, 1950) handed over the lands to the landless. This, Datta stresses, was a step in the right direction and helped promote agriculture. But, it was changed soon by setting up agricultural co-operatives and communes, where the peasants were denied ownership of land. This retarded agricultural growth.

The commune reduced the peasants to agricultural labourers. Everything belonged to the people, that is the State. The State promised to look after every need of the people. The State was responsible for everything. For individuals, there was hardly any incentive, either to produce or to earn more. The communes represented a classic case of the state being responsible for everything, but in the end, no one was responsible for the state. The method of distribution of income in the commune was always under dispute and a uniform method could not satisfy all. The income in the communes differed as a result of the factor endowment of the region. This created inter-personal inequality in income and consumption.

The policy of "Grain as a Key Link" explicitly stated that the production teams should first produce grain to meet the needs of its members and then should venture in other areas of agriculture. Such a policy was squarely responsible for stagnation in agricultural production. Commercial crops were neglected as the communes were not allowed to cultivate them before meeting their food grain demand. The discussion on rice and wheat has been drawn to show that the Chinese were perhaps late in introducing modern varieties of wheat.

The growth of foodgrain output (in China foodgrain includes potato, corn, millet and other coarse grains besides rice and wheat, which most commentators ignore even now) shows that the initial spur following land reform was great by contemporary standards. Afterwards, it slowed down consistently. A three-year average, to eliminate yearly fluctuation shows that per capita foodgrain consumption declined from 197 kilogram in 1952-54 to 192.5 kilogram in 1976-78. Foodgrain production was neither balanced nor stable; it did not have even a reasonable capacity to withstand the aberrations of nature. In 1978, the foodgrain production was such that the country had to import about 4 per cent of its consumption in a normal agricultural year.

The distribution mechanism was not able to wipe out the inequality in food consumption, but it prevented food consumption from falling below a minimum where people are threatened with acute hunger and malnutrition, except in unusually bad years. This however, was no mean achievement because, many developing countries, with similar per capita income were not able to provide what China could, to its people at large.

Two-third of the population was estimated as poor in 1978. The official estimate, made at a much later date is : one-third of the population. This difference is due to the choice of the poverty line. Datta uses per capita annual income of 150 yuan as the poverty line, used by research scholars in the late 1970s and early 1980s, while the official estimate later was 100 yuan. He estimates one-third of the people in extreme poverty - under two-third of the poverty line (100 yuan – the official poverty line).

The estimates of calorie deficient population is derived on the basis of a methodology developed in an earlier paper by Datta. If it is assumed that the intake of calories is perfectly equal, then the entire population is calorie deficient and everyone's deficit is 23 per cent. With inequality in calorie intake, the percentage of calorie deficient population reduces (from 100 per cent) but it drives the rest to a greater deficiency (more than 23 per cent). Regional inequality in the variables that dictate the levels of living and quality of life, increased in central plan era.

China, Datta shows, is implementing economic reform programmes in a step-by-step approach and not following the programmes of IMF in toto. They apply the programmes in limited areas; test their efficacy, and depending on the results, extend these to wider areas.

The equilibrating role of market is a concern for China though efficiency and economic growth topped the agenda. It's traditional concern about social problems arising from market mechanism made them extremely careful in deregulating markets. The trade-off between efficiency gains out of the functioning of the market and social problems forced them to pursue the reforms programmes in a step-by-step approach and careful in deregulating markets. In view of the vastness of the country and its varying levels of spatial development, they considered unwise to apply a uniform strategy throughout the country.

This important book is essential reading for Sinophiles, economists and development practitioners.

Thaltej
Ahmedabad
July 15, 2003

YOGINDER K. ALAGH
Ex-Minister of State for Planning,
Programme Implementation,
Power and Science and Technology
(Independent Charge)
Government of India.

Preface

Central planning is now a matter of history. Excessive state control on the means of production and distribution can be identified as the main reason for its failure. Soviet Union and People's Republic of China are its worst victims.

The People's Republic of China founded in 1949 by the Chinese Communist Party viewed central planning as a route to attain the goals of Marxism, though its efficacy in maximizing the rate of economic growth and ensuring all-round development was not clearly established.

The high rate of economic growth experienced by China in the early years of the Republic, caused by low base and latent energy, was mistaken as the miracle of central planning. The illusion should have been over by early 1960s when the major macro- and socio-economic variables began to stagnate. However, the search for an alternative strategy was on before 1970, for, the Chinese with a huge population and little resources could not afford the luxury of the Soviet Union to carry on.

How central planning led to stagnation of the Chinese economy and how deep the stagnation was? This is probed here with the statistics officially released by the Chinese authorities.

The origin of this study can be traced to thirteen months leave granted to me by the Government of India way back in 1987 to accompany my wife and daughter to Glasgow, Scotland. For this, I am grateful to Professor S. R. Hashim, then Adviser in the Planning Commission. The leave was not granted for this study specifically; it was to take care of our daughter so that my wife can pursue her studies. Clearly, I was underemployed. At this juncture, Radha Sinha, then Professor at Glasgow University, arranged the research facilities for this study in Glasgow University. I am grateful to Professor Sinha for all the help. My wife tolerated my busy and irregular schedule that accompanied this research. For this, I am grateful to her.

The study could not be completed during the stay in Glasgow. The opportunity seemed near after six years when I was posted in the Planning Commission. But my elevated position there came in the way; then the Ninth Five Year Plan. To compound the delay, the Ninth Plan had to be prepared twice, as the political leadership at the Federal Government changed.

As the dust settled and I was about to open the China papers towards the beginning of 2000, Savita Sharma, Director, who assumed the charge on Poverty in 1985, reminded me about the documents she has been keeping with her for so long. My head with China and heart with poverty, delayed the work by another two years; but a study - Facets of Indian Poverty – was complete and I could begin the unfinished work on China. In this period, I have been helped by many friends and colleagues. I am grateful to Dr Pronab Sen, Adviser, Planning Commission and Professor Bibek Debroy, Director, Rajiv Gandhi Foundation, New Delhi, for the discussions I had with them. I respond to the regular enquiries from my daughter, Amrita, now a grown up girl, about the progress of the study and occasional offer of assistance, with a thank-you for the display of concern and gesture. The errors and omissions, however, rest with me.

The original study was restricted to first five chapters for which the source of information are given in the reference at the end. The chapter on economic reforms is an afterthought. The data on China used in this chapter are drawn from the Statistical Year Book of China, 2001.

K.L. DATTA

Contents

List of Tables

Introduction

The tide of the socialist countries that had radiated outwards from the Soviet Union to China is over. The central reason behind the collapse of the socialist economies is central planning, which was imposed on both resource-rich and resource-starved countries, and also on countries with population of high and low densities. It failed everywhere.

China is a country of relatively little resources compared to its population, and Russia is a country with a smaller population compared to its huge resources. Both these countries took the route of central planning to a wished success. It took quarter of a century for the Chinese to realise its adverse impact on the economy. But, pragmatic as they are, tackled the problems at the stagnation stage and saved themselves from falling into a catastrophe unlike its Russian and east-European comrades, who went beyond and pursued the course even at the stagnation stage. They ultimately had to change when the stagnation prolonged into a decline. The extent and depth of stagnation in the Chinese economy as an offshoot of central planning, and the manner in which stagnation crept into, are unfolded here in a purely development perspective and economic sense.

The development process in China in the initial years of the People's Republic (1949-1957) is marked by a high rate of economic growth caused mainly by two factors. These are low base and latent energy, both of which are known to have a short duration. As the economy moves into a higher growth path, the base becomes larger and the growth rate correspondingly lower. The latent energy fritters away quickly and requires timely replacement by an efficient system based on adequate material incentive. Personal incentive had very little or no place under central planning and a major part of the income was distributed on the basis of welfare rather than productivity criteria. This neither produced growth nor resulted in equity.

The issue of development is instinctively correlated with growth. First, the economy should attain a reasonable rate of income growth. This income, as far as possible, should be distributed equally among the population. This makes participation of most of the population, if not all, in the growth process important. The growth process in China under central planning was participatory to the extent that the endeavour was not to leave anyone outside the process of income generation, though a vast majority were underemployed. The aim was also to generate an income profile, which is egalitarian to the core. But, the differential productivity of land created a kind of income inequality in the countryside, which the growth process failed to check. The concept of egalitarianism was imposed rigorously on a low rate of growth and the development strategy under central planning lay in the labyrinth of growth-equity nexus. The trade-off between growth and equity in charting out the course of economic development very often came to be synonymous with the conflict between the egalitarian policies and material incentives.

A direct nexus between work and remuneration is considered as the essential propelling mechanism in the growth process. Absence of this nexus in central planning is inter-woven with the pricing mechanism and inter-sectoral allocation of resources. Prices were not linked to costs resulting in a "scissors gap". The state through the monopoly it enjoyed in the marketing of input and output, kept the prices of industrial products at a level higher than that of agricultural products, forcing the farmers to pay higher price for the industrial products, which they have to buy, and receive lower prices for agricultural products, which they produce and sell. This gap between the prices of agricultural and industrial products is known as "scissors gap" as, from an equilibrium point, these two prices like the two blades of a scissor, move in opposite direction. Centrally planned countries in their early stages of development have used this mechanism to transfer rural resources for industrial development. The model of economic development adopted by the Soviet Union in the early 1920s is an example.

The inter-sectoral allocation of resources was rarely consistent, resulting in mismatch between demand and supply. The market forces were not free and competitive so as to ensure efficient utilization of resources, both material and non-material. Through central planning the State imposed an output structure on the economy, which often was not market clearing. This created disequilibria in factor and product markets and came in the way of allocative efficiency.

Agricultural operations in China under central planning were directly controlled and regulated by the State. In comparison, the State in neighbouring India confined its activities in agriculture to the creation of infrastructure, subsidising farm inputs and regulating prices, leaving the production decisions to millions of farmers in the countryside. The farmers' produce in the private sector picking up price and fiscal signals from the State. The State intervenes in the market during bumper years by mopping up surplus farm produce to prevent a fall in its prices. It also takes care of the interests of the consumers by pumping in farm products in the market to contain the prices at affordable level. Indian agriculture operated under a market system, which is free but not "free for all" as the State had a say in its development and was always in search of ways and means to make the least but the most effective intervention in the market. Through this *modus operandi,* Indian agriculture generated surplus production in the market without any proven evidence of increase in inequality in the distribution of agricultural income. It is also spared from food imports, which is a sensitive issue in any developing country. In contrast, the foodgrain production in China stagnated in the absence of a market mechanism, which can balance the interests of producers and consumers.

The economic policies (and for that matter, all policies) in China were discussed within a camarilla. This was punctuated by a controlled Press, which was used more as a publicity machine and less as a forum for discussion and debate. The fall-out of the policies at every stage of development needs brainstorming debate not only within but also outside the government. A free Press being an integral part of the development process can play a positive role. China paid a heavy price for controlled Press particularly during the Great Leap Forward (1958-61).

Even in democratic countries sometimes, Press has been gagged *albeit* with enormous cost. An example, again from India, where the Press is famous for highlighting failures and sinking economic stories. Since the founding of the Republic in 1950, India enjoys a free Press except for a brief (19-month) period (June 1975 to January 1977) of internal emergency. It's price was heavy as bureaucrats and politicians took advantage of the censorship and often acted contrary to government policies without the fear of being reported. A free Press may sometimes create white noise or carry opinions of individuals or groups managing it, but its existence prevents people particularly in high places to take a free hand.

The focus here is on the strategy of economic development in China under the aegis of central planning and its outcome. On attaining liberation in October 1949 after a prolonged armed struggle, a disjoint and fragmented economy was consolidated. By 1952, the transport and communication network, which was severely disrupted during the civil war, was restored. A rampant inflation ever witnessed in the country was brought under control, making it ready to usher in an era of planned economic development. The country launched its First Five Year Plan in the following year. China's tryst with central planning ended in the Third Plenary Session of the Eleventh Central Committee of the Chinese

Communist Party held in December 1978. The assessment of the economy under central planning thus has to be for the period 1952-78.

This study consists of six chapters. The first chapter summarises the growth and development strategy adopted during the period 1952-78 and outlines its principal consequences. Considering the role of agriculture in a low income, land scarce economy, the agricultural strategy and its outcome is assessed in Chapter 2. The communes, which formed the backbone of rural development under central planning is the subject matter of Chapter 3. The incidence of poverty and inequality has been assessed in Chapter 4 and the regional differential in major macro-economic variables in Chapter 5. These can ideally take stock of the central planning in its pursuit of raising the level of income, employment and output and consequently the levels of living and quality of life.

The dismantling of the central planning apparatus began in 1979 with the introduction of policies of economic reform and liberalization whose hallmark is market mechanism, replacing the different agents of the government as decision makers. The state began to withdraw from the economic sectors allowing space to the private sector and took upon itself the responsibility of creating suitable environment for growth and development instead of directly participating in production and distribution. In the era of economic reform, planning was not abolished altogether. It was used in some form, particularly in agriculture and infrastructure sector. The economic reform did not rule out the necessity of planning in order to identify inter-sectoral constraints, to take a stock of the resources, to indicate the methods by which these resources can be augmented in a sustained manner and to guide government policy action. Of all, some kind of planning is vital to identify the emerging vulnerabilities arising from the uncertainties that accompany the market based system and to suggest measures to address them. However, the manner and method of state intervention in the economy through planning, in short the planning methodology during the economic reform was different from the central planning era due to the significant reduction in the instruments available to the state to control the economic matters. The state intervened through planning only to tend the market for the best interests of the country.

The implementation of the policies of economic reform and liberalization in China during the past two decades has been watched with great interest. Its outcome at every stage has been monitored and evaluated from various angles within and outside the country. At this backdrop, Chapter 6 outlines the course of reforms with its salient features. This may also serve as a comparison between the central planning and the market-led development in China.

1

Growth and Development

The People's Republic of China dominates the Third World in terms of population and area. Its land border with more than a dozen countries such as Mongolia in the north, Russia and North Korea in the north-east, Myanmar, Laos and Vietnam in the south, India, Nepal and Bhutan in south-west and Afghanistan, Tajikistan, Kyrgyz Republic and Kazakhstan in the west, underlines its strategic importance. However, on the basis of per capita income, the World Bank classified China as a low-income developing country in 1978, when it bid good-bye to central planning.

I
The Setting

The end of World War II witnessed de-colonisation and birth of a number of independent nations in Asia, Africa and Latin America. The low level of development in these countries created awareness about the problems of achieving high rate of economic growth and the concern for faster percolation of the fruits of economic growth to the poorer sections of the society. A majority of these countries adopted some form of market economy in which the state played an active role to promote economic growth and development through planning. In fact, planning became the password for orderly progress in these less developed countries. Some countries joined the socialist block and adopted central planning where the state directly controlled the means of production and distribution. Central planning was at the heart of the Chinese development strategy.

A Closed Economy ?

China was not recognized by the United Nations until 1971. It was in October 1971, at its twenty-sixth session (1967th Plenary Meeting), that the United Nations General Assembly adopted a Resolution (No. 2758) in which it recognized the People's Republic of China as the only legitimate representative of China to the United Nations and in all the organizations related to it. Until then, China was also not recognized by the United States of America and most of the developed capitalist countries of Western Europe, *inter alia* the members of the North Atlantic Treaty Organization (NATO). The first state level contact between China and the United States surfaced from the secret visit of Henry Kissenger, then Assistant to the President for National Affairs, to Beijing in 1971. The President of the United States of America paid an official visit to China in 1972. The two countries had set up liaison offices in each other's capitals in 1973. But, the diplomatic relation was formally established from the New Year Day, 1979 and the first trade agreement was signed six months later.

From this isolation of first two decades of the existence of the People's Republic, originated the widely held notion that it was a closed economy. May be it was in some respect, but not entirely. China was recognized by the erstwhile Soviet Union on the very day it was proclaimed as People's Republic. The East European countries followed suit. By the early 1950s, China established trade relations with forty countries. With the improvement of the relations with West European countries and the establishment of diplomatic relation with the European Economic Community in 1975, China's trading partners increased to 156 countries.[1] Notably, many of these were capitalist countries and countries ruled by military dictators. The trade relations and economic interests were meticulously separated from the class and form of government of the trading partner and were written on the drawing board of economics.

The flow of foreign assistance in the initial years was significant. The People's Republic of China and the erstwhile Soviet Union signed a thirty years Treaty of Friendship, Alliance, and Mutual Assistance in 1950. A number of agreements on economic and technical co-operation projects were signed under this treaty in 1953 and 1954. These projects were to form the core of the First Five Year Plan. These assistances were not in bits and pieces as most of the low income developing countries usually receive from technologically advanced countries. These came in the form of complete plant and machinery, embracing the entire industry and infrastructure, installed and put into operation under the aegis of Soviet experts. In the 1950s, East European countries and the Soviet Union constructed more than four hundred large-scale projects in sectors covering electrical, metallurgical, petroleum, telecommunications, coal, chemical, iron and steel, mining, non-ferrous metals, machine building and power. In the First Plan, Poland, Bulgaria, East Germany and Czechoslovakia assisted in 68 key projects.[2]

The bonhomie with the Soviet Union did not last long. Soviet assistance was terminated somewhat abruptly in July 1960 with the recalling of all of their 1390 experts then working in China along with the blue prints and technical data. As a result, a large number of specialised contracts and scientific and technical co-operation projects were scrapped. Trade as a consequence, switched to developing and developed market economies, and by 1962, imports of technology commenced from Western Europe and Japan, a process, which was accelerated in the early 1970s with the improvement of relation with the United States of America and the European Economic Community. Between 1972 and 1977, 222 plants were imported from 19 countries including Japan, Britain, France, the Netherlands, United States of America and West Germany. The direction of trade by the late 1970s shifted to the capitalist countries, with which 90 percent of total trade was transacted in 1979; its 25.2 percent of total imports were from Japan, 21.3 percent from European Economic Community and 11.9 percent from the United States of America.[3] Meanwhile, Soviet loans were reimbursed by 1966. This repayment strained the domestic resource position and was one of the factors behind the retardation of the rate of economic growth at this time.

Table 1.1: Trade Elasticity

No.	*Item*	*1960-1978*	*1952-1978*
1.	Export	1.063	0.906
2.	Import	1.280	0.814
3.	Total Trade	1.165	0.856

Notes: 1. The elasticities are with respect to national income and estimated using log-log function.
2. Estimated from the data in *Statistical Yearbook of China*, State Statistical Bureau, Beijing, 1986, pp. 40 and 481.

The growth rate of total trade is 9.35 percent per year in 1952-60 and 4.59 percent per year in 1960-78. The high growth until 1960 is mainly due to a low base and the low growth in post 1960s may partly be explained by the Soviet withdrawal. As in most large economies, the trade-national income ratio in China was low; total trade was about 2 percent of the national income until the 1960s. But, during the period 1960-78, the elasticity of total trade with respect to national income is greater than unity and import elasticity is greater than export elasticity. The trade elasticity given in Table 1.1 does not portray the picture of a closed economy.

The Process of Central Control

Planning in China was greatly influenced by regulation of economic activities, based on central control of the means of production and distribution. The entire modern transport sector and about one-third of the industrial enterprises were already under state supervision before the establishment of the People's Republic in 1949. These were nationalized and made state-owned enterprises. The remaining industries, which were in the private sector, were brought under state control within the next few years. The origin of industrial output given in Table 1.2 shows that central control on industry was firmly established even before the First Five-Year Plan commenced as private enterprises accounted for only 17.1 percent of industrial output in 1952. By 1956, private enterprises were abolished and the State gained absolute control of industry as the share of state enterprises in industrial output was 67.5 percent and the remaining 32.5 percent originated in joint-state private enterprise, which carried out production as per requirement of state plan.

The monetary system was placed firmly under government control well before 1952. The commercial banks were nationalized and the banking system was brought under central control with the People's Bank of China as the central bank of the country.

The state took over the responsibility of trading. Its share in 1952 was 63.7 percent in wholesale trade and 42.6 percent in retail trade. The State monopolised marketing of several items of daily necessities such as foodgrain, edible oil and cotton fabrics and restricted the scope of activity of private traders by placing order directly with private processing and manufacturing enterprises. The state monopoly in marketing of commodities, known as unified planning and differentiated control was shaped in the following way. First, thirty eight items of basic necessities including foodgrain, edible oils and cotton fabrics were controlled directly by the state. In the second category, 293 items were identified for domestic consumption and export. These include pork, beef, mutton, egg, tobacco, wine, and essential consumer durables. The state regulated their supply and distribution. The provincial governments were allowed to adopt their own regulatory mechanism in respect of the remaining items. As a result, by 1954, the state commerce department and supply and marketing co-operatives raised their share to 90 percent of wholesale trade leaving only 10 percent with the private sector. In order to strengthen market control and ensure supply of basic necessities, the state took over the entire trade and commerce by 1956 through establishment of specialised national corporations, supplemented by its regional subsidiaries. Thus, a unified marketing mechanism was established with public ownership of the means of production and distribution, reducing the role of the market as auxiliary.

Table 1.2: Origin of Industrial Output

(*Percentage*)

	Ownership Type	*1949*	*1952*	*1956*
1.	State	34.7	56.0	67.5
2.	Joint State-Private	9.5	26.9	32.5
3.	Private	55.8	17.1	0.0
	Total	100.0	100.0	100.0

Source: Xue Muquio. *China's Socialist Economy,* Foreign Languages Press, Beijing. 1981, pp. 19, 22 and 29.

Subsequently, the state take-over of the means of production and distribution was shaped in two forms. These are: (a) state ownership, known as ownership of the whole people, and (b) collective ownership, which are the industries under the communes. Under the ownership of the whole people came the large industries, which were commonly known as state-owned industries. These were mostly basic and key industries and represented the leading force of the national economy. The operational control and effective ownership of state-owned enterprises belonged to either the central government or the provincial government, including autonomous regions or the municipalities with independent planning status. In some cases, the management and control of these industries were shared jointly by any of the above administration. Some of the medium sized state-owned enterprises were managed by the provincial and sub-provincial level administration at the city or the county level. The industries under collective ownership were generally small-scale units using little machinery and mostly labour intensive techniques of production, located in both rural and urban areas and managed by either the city or the commune administration. The activities of both the state-owned industries and the industries under collective ownership were geared to requirement of the state via the state plan.

II
The Planning Process

The public ownership of the means of production and distribution made planning as fundamental to the integrated and balanced sectoral development of the economy. The role of planning in the development process is enshrined in the Constitution as: "the State by means of economic planning directs development and transformation of national economy, tries to increase productive capacity constantly so as to improve the living standard of the people."[4] Planning embraced every aspect of economic activity and development process of the economy, and was expected to place the country to the pinnacle of prosperity and influence.

The planning process in the People's Republic was initiated in 1950 with the setting up of Planning Bureau, which then formed a part of the Financial and Economic Commission. It was engaged mainly in annual planning exercises. The State Planning Commission was set up in November 1952. The formulation of the national plan, integrating production, distribution, consumption and accumulation, each with various economic activities, spread across the regions, was its job. The State Economic Commission was carved out in May 1956 from the existing State Planning Commission in order to formulate annual plans. State Planning Commission retained the charge of perspective planning. The planning machinery at provincial and county level was also constituted to meet the exigencies of decentralised planning and by 1956 each of the two thousand counties in the country constituted their own planning machinery.

The State Planning Commission

The State Planning Commission was constituted with a chairman, eight vice-chairmen, eleven members and one thousand and five hundred staff. There were 21 major divisions of the State Planning Commission in June 1956. These are: (a) Overall planning, (b) Long range planning, (c) Heavy industry, (d) Fuel, (e) Machine building, (f) Defence industry, (g) Light industry and textile, (h) Overall industrial production, (i) Agriculture and water conservancy, (j) Transport and communication, (k) Domestic trade, (l) Foreign trade, (m) Culture, education and health, (n) Training and placement of technical personnel, (o) Wages and employment, (p) Cost of production and prices, (q) Finance and banking, (r) Allocation of means of production between State enterprises, (s) Allocation of machinery and electrical equipment, (t) Overall planning for capital construction, and (u) Stocks of essential material. The major responsibilities of the divisions are outlined below.

Overall planning division prepares the annual plan. It later came under the Economic Commission. Long range planning division is responsible for sectoral plans and their integration with the national plan. Heavy industry division is in charge of iron and steel, non-ferrous metals, chemicals and building equipments. Coal, copper, electricity and petroleum are under fuel industry. Heavy machinery, machine tools, automobiles, tractor, locomotive and shipbuilding come under machine building industry. Industries related with manufacture of machinery required for defence are placed under defence industry. The principal task of overall industrial production division is to coordinate plans of various industries and to ensure equilibrium between capital goods and consumer goods. Agriculture and water conservancy division formulates production planning of grain crop, harnessing of river and development of State farm. The main endeavour of trade division is to meet the requirement of consumption goods. It also lays down production targets keeping in view the purchasing power of the people. Export, import and balance of payments rest with foreign trade division, which also sets the direction of trade. Wages and employment division prepares employment plans, determines wage level and monitors labour productivity. Pricing of products and prices fixed by the State for trading between government departments and agencies are task of cost of production and prices division. Trade division determines market price. Finance and banking division is concerned with accumulation of capital. The division in charge of stocks is primarily responsible for maintaining inventory of essential goods.

The fundamental task of national economic planning boils down to determination of the ratio between: (a) production and consumption, (b) consumption and accumulation, (c) output of means of production and means of consumption, (d) industrial and agricultural production, and consequently to set the parametric values of: (i) labour force in relation to material resources and (ii) average wage in relation to growth of labour productivity, (e) circulating goods and monetary income, (f) various regions, and (g) various economic elements.

The Governor usually heads the planning organisation in the county. It functions under the provincial Planning Commission, which, in turn, is guided by the State Planning Commission. The primary responsibility of the county level planning organisation is to: (a) formulate plans within its jurisdiction and promulgate targets, (b) carry out instructions issued by the State, (c) exploit local resources, and (d) supervise and implement the plans.

The Plan was implemented through the state budget. The state budget consisted of the budgets of the central government, including the state owned industrial enterprises and the budgets of the provincial governments.

The Model

The planning models usually play two roles. First, it defines the strategy of development, i.e., it solves the choice between agriculture and industry; within industry, between heavy and light industry, between capital and consumer goods, etc. Second, it assesses the various economic (and social as well) parameters and determines targets, which are consistent with the available resources and also are inter-sectorally consistent.

China began with a straightforward application of the model of economic development adopted by the Soviet Union in its early years of the Bolshevik Revolution in the 1920s. It was based on extracting surplus from agriculture to finance the investment in heavy industry. This model of economic development was characterised by high degree of centralisation and administrative regulation, neatly fastened to public ownership of the means of production and distribution. For China, it was translated into rigid restrictions on state enterprises and collective economic organisations.

The First Plan (1953-57) aimed to build the foundation of a strong industrial base. It planned for 694 "above-norm" projects including 156 mega projects.[5] The definition of mega project is normative and was associated with investment, which varies between industry and category of project. Investment between two and ten million Yuan in heavy industry and three and five million Yuan in light industry are defined as "above-norm". The development strategy witnessed a change in 1958 when the Second Five-Year Plan was about to commence. The signs of change were already in the air with the announcement of "Ten Major Relationships" in 1956, which delineated the sectoral interrelations keeping in view the domestic compulsions. The planning process accorded emphasis on the relationships between:

(a) agriculture and industry and within industry, between heavy and light industry,
(b) industry in coastal region and in interior,
(c) economic construction and defence requirement,
(d) State sector and individual in the domain of production, and
(e) the centre and the regions.

These relations while underlining the growth path of the economy, acknowledge that economic growth alone is not sufficient to ensure social justice. The trade-off between growth and equity can be traced here in the Chinese context. It marks a departure from the Soviet model of economic development no doubt, but not from central planning and the associated control and regulation of the means of production and distribution. It was still a "top-down" approach in which a highly centralised state apparatus exercised detail control over economic policy through enormous Ministries in the capital city, Beijing, and pursued until 1978, barring the period of Great Leap Forward, which after about an year's flurry of activities beginning mid-1958 sank into oblivion. However, for the underlying reasons behind the formulation of the Great Leap Forward and also for the kind of aberrations the Great Leap created in the economy it would be appropriate to have a look at its salient features, including some of the results.

Great Leap Forward

Economics in socialist countries is generally dominated by politics. The Great Leap Forward is politics with slogans from economics. The Great Leap was conceived after the conclusion of the first plan and its general line was announced at the Second Session of the Eighth Party Congress in May 1958.

The Great Leap Forward was born out of a fear and a faith. The fear originated from the long-term implications of Soviet assistance on the Chinese economy, particularly in terms of economic dependence. The faith was purely subjective and took the shape of a conviction that there was scope of more efficient utilization of the domestic resources, which coupled with latent energy, can produce simultaneous development of industry and agriculture at a much faster rate. The former led to abandoning the Soviet model of economic development in its original form and formulating a kind of grass-root planning, for which a new socio-economic order was to be created in the countryside. The latter, that is the conviction of a faster growth of the economy was viewed as a pursuit of maximization of the growth rates in industry and agriculture.

The re-structuring of the socio-economic relations in the

countryside began with the formation of the communes. Within three months of the announcement of the Great Leap, the agricultural co-operatives in the countryside were re-organised into communes. Most of the agricultural projects exceeded the administrative boundary of a single co-operative, giving rise to management problems. Based on the idea that their merger would lead to optimal solution, the agricultural co-operatives then numbering little less than three-quarter of a million were re-organised into 23630 communes in August 1958. The second plan fixed the target growth rates of agriculture and industry as 6.1 percent per year and 10 percent per year respectively. The Great Leap Forward raised these targets to 16.8 percent per year in agriculture and 33 percent per year in industry, simply with the faith that the country can grow more. The situation reached preposterous proportions in case of iron and steel for which the target was doubled from 5.35 million tonnes set in the second plan to 10.7 million tonnes.

The communes as the epicenter of the process of social transformation, particularly of the rural society, were conceived in the Great Leap Forward. Under its various programmes, a great deal of inter-sectoral transfer of manpower took place. Many agricultural workers were transferred from farming to commune industries or in irrigation or hydroelectric projects in the rural areas. Some flow of manpower also took place from urban to rural areas, mainly in order to streamline the commune administration. The government had already passed a series of laws for the emancipation of women and to prevent any form of discrimination based on gender. Yet, a majority of them were confined to housekeeping. In the process of social transformation, this traditional role of women in the society was to be re-written, ensuring conducive atmosphere for their participation in the developmental activities, *en masse*. The community kitchens where the commune members were to take their meals compulsorily were introduced precisely keeping this in view. Conceived originally as a part of the policy of food distribution, the aim was also to free the women from household chores in order to enable them to participate fully in the economic and political activities, which hitherto was considered a male bastion. The food in the community kitchens may be luscious but the project failed to take off perhaps as people considered their regular meals a private affair and best enjoyed with family members.

Planning at the end of the day is a matter of construction of a series of alternatives by a team of competent and qualified experts, placed before the political authorities who make the choice among these alternatives. The Great Leap Forward bears the evidence of disastrous consequences that a country can experience when the plan is framed by the political authorities. The Great Leap Forward involved an enormous amount of experimentation. As it had no detailed blueprint except a few underlying strategic principles, it ended in an economic failure. Partly as a result of the utilization of the latent energy and partly as the industrial plants under construction during the First Five Year Plan went to steam, the industrial production in 1958 rose significantly as compared to the previous year. But in the next two years the industrial production declined; the annual rate of decline touched a double digit figure. The industry either suffered from shortages of raw materials or was burdened with inventory goods of inferior quality. A similar increase in agricultural production also took place in 1958, partly aided by favourable weather and partly by use of latent energy. The commune system being egalitarian to the core in the matter of distribution of income, was initially favoured by a vast majority of the rural population who were either landless or owned little land. But, the agricultural production in 1959 being greatly affected by unfavourable weather and natural calamity, declined significantly. Besides, it was discovered that the reported agricultural production estimates for 1958 were highly exaggerated by the statistical agencies of the newly established rural organizations. The figures generated by theses agencies were born out of zeal rather than facts and theory. The drop in agricultural output in 1959 resulted in substantial food shortage, culminating in widespread hunger and famine in the rural areas. The cost of this failure was high; Mao Zedong, the undisputed leader of the country and the architect of the Great Leap Forward, accepting moral responsibility of the failure, resigned from his position of the Chairman of the People's Republic in April, 1959. He, however, remained the Chairman of the Chinese Communist Party (CCP).

III
Growth and Structure of the Economy

Growth

The growth of the economy is measured by changes in the national income. There are two methods of calculating national income in China. First, it is calculated as the sum total of net value of output of material production sectors. Agriculture, industry, construction, transport and communication are known as the material production sectors. The net (value of) output is obtained by subtracting the value of material consumption and depreciation of fixed asset from gross (value of) output. Material consumption is the input use of the material production sectors. It includes: (a) raw and finished material, such as, fuel, power, seed, feed etc., (b) cost of transport, (c) cost of processing of semi-finished products contracted to other enterprises, (d) repairing cost, and (e) depreciation of fixed asset. In the second approach, national income is calculated as the sum of wage, profit, tax and interest in the above mentioned five material production sectors.

The total product is a measure of the value of output. It is the sum total of gross value of output of the five abovementioned material production sectors. The gross output is equivalent to the sum total of net output and input use including depreciation of capital stock. The material product is produced directly by agriculture, industry and construction while transport and commerce create and add value to the product.

National income is used to measure the growth performance of the economy in preference to total product since total product may rise exclusively due to rise in input use. The sectoral growth rates of national income and total product and their sectoral shares are given in Table 1.3. The overall rate of economic growth measured by national income is 5.24 percent per year in 1952-78. The population growth was about two per cent per year. Thus, per capita income rose by three and a quarter per cent. The sectoral growth rates of total product are higher than national income, symbolising rising input coefficient and an inefficient production structure, arising from declining marginal productivity of capital.

Table 1.3: National Income and Total Product: Growth in 1952-78

(Per cent per year)

Sector	*National Income*		*Total Product*	
1. Agriculture	2.31	(-0.96)	3.11	(-1.61)
2. Industry	9.30	(2.59)	9.34	(1.66)
3. Construction	5.36	(0)	6.99	(0)
4. Transport	5.18	(-0.93)	5.76	(-1.16)
5. Commerce	2.76	(-2.69)	3.51	(-2.70)
Total	5.24		6.75	

Note: These are trend growth rates, estimated from exponential time function. The figures in brackets are trend growth rates of sectoral share.

Source: Estimated from the data in *Statistical Yearbook of China,* State Statistical Bureau. Beijing, different issues, 1981 to 1986.

Structural Change

The growth of national income brought about structural changes in the economy. The share of agriculture in both national income and total product reduced while that of industry rose. The falling share of agriculture was witnessed amidst extraordinary fluctuations; its reason being the inability of the agriculture to withstand natural calamities causing drastic fall in output in abnormal years.

The increased share of industry in national income was not translated into employment generation and increase in real wage. It also bypassed the disposable income of rural population. As a result in 1978, (a) agriculture remained as the mainstay of rural income; (b) productive income in rural areas constituted 92 percent of total income and only 8 percent came from non-productive sources such as collective accumulation and public welfare fund, state budget and personal income transfer; (c) agriculture, and allied activities such as farming, forestry, fishery, animal husbandry, generated 85 percent of total income and 92.4 percent of productive income; (d) only 7.6 percent of productive income in rural areas came from non-agricultural activities such as, rural industry, transport, communication and trade.

A greater part of the dependence of rural income on agriculture is due to the wide variation in relative prices of agriculture and industry, whose reason lay centered in the price system in a centrally planned economy, which being determined by the state, rather than the market neither reflect real cost nor do serve, as in a market economy, as signals to producer of goods to plan their production. It is mainly used as an instrument to reconcile the total demand of consumer goods with the supply, allowing for revenues to the State.

The share of trade and commerce in national income declined between 1952 and 1978. The share of commerce in national income was low due to the state takeover of trade and commerce and large proportion of self-consumption in rural areas. The decline in the share of transport in national income at the background of high industrial growth may be explained by the growth of specific localised industries, where transport linkage does not arise at all. The restriction on internal movement of rural population (constituting 90 percent of the total population) both within rural areas and from rural to urban areas, effected through the household registration system may also be a reason. Finally, the structural changes in the economy surface slower growth and consequently a weak tertiary sector whereas a typical developing economy generally experience a growing tertiary sector. The growth pattern bypassed the services sector. To put it in proper perspective, the growth was set to by pass the services sector as it was considered unproductive.

IV
Consumption *vs.* Accumulation

The national income can be decomposed into consumption and accumulation. Consumption is of two types, *viz.*, private (or personal) and public (or Government). Private consumption is the value of goods and services purchased, or received in kind, by households. It includes items of daily use besides food and clothing, and their level dictates the standard of living of the people. Public consumption is the expenditure on government administration, defence etc. Accumulation is that part of national income which is spent for productive and non-productive construction. It is synonymous with investment in a market economy.

Investment is essential for economic growth. An increased consumption lowers investment, and hence the economic growth. On the contrary, an increased accumulation reduces private consumption but creates a base from where the economy can be poised for steady growth. A choice on the ratio of consumption and accumulation in national income is crucial as the exigency of long-term growth and development solicits a balance between the two.

Accumulation Rate and Economic Growth

Accumulation as percentage to national income (known as accumulation rate), increased from 20-22 percent in the early 1950s to 30-35 percent in the 1970s. During the period 1953 to 1979, the accumulation rate was:

(a) less than 20% in three years,
(b) between 20% and 25% in ten years, and
(c) greater than 30% in fourteen years.

The nexus between accumulation rate and economic growth can be viewed from the following:

(a) *First Plan (1953-57)*: The accumulation rate in the First Plan period ranged from 22 to 25 per cent. For the five year period, it averaged 24.8 per cent. This low accumulation rate in the first plan had a favourable impact on income growth and level of living as it realized an annual increase of 8.9 percent in national income, 10.9 per cent in industrial and agricultural output and 7.4 per cent in wages.
(b) *Second Plan (1958-62)*: Average accumulation rate was 40 percent in the first three years of the Second Plan. The decline in the national income in the last two years of the Second Plan forced a decline in the accumulation rate. It was necessary to maintain a threshold level of consumption. In the Second Plan, the accumulation rate averaged 31.6 per cent and the industrial and agricultural output increased by 0.8 per cent per annum and national income declined by 3.1 per cent per annum. The high

accumulation rate in the Second Plan is believed to have distorted the inter-sectoral balance. The standard of living deteriorated and acute food shortage resulted in widespread hunger in which several millions in the countryside died of famine. Chinese reports at this time did not mention these deaths and merely mentioned existence of malnutrition and occasionally starvation. The official estimate calculated at a later stage from the increase in mortality rate during the period 1958-61 from its normal level (mortality rate in 1957) placed the number of deaths to 15 million people. This estimate, however, is seriously disputed. Dreze and Sen, quoting several studies based on Chinese data stated: "the famines of 1958-61 killed, it appears, between 23 and 30 million people. Peng estimated 23 million extra deaths. The estimate of Ashton and others is close to 30 million."[6]

(c) *Readjustment Period (1963-65)*: The accumulation rate in these three years averaged 22.8 percent. The approach in this period is stylised as "readjustment, consolidation, filling out and improvement". The rectification of sectoral imbalance in the economy caused by proportionately higher investment in capital construction projects (*i.e.*, construction of factories, mines, railroads, waterworks, bridges, hospitals, educational institutions, etc.), to build up fixed assets, and in heavy industry is known as "readjustment". The policy of "consolidation" means fusing the gains of economic development. Completion of the projects initiated earlier and particularly during the Great Leap Forward is termed as "filling out". The emphasis on efficiency, technological upgradation and quality of production is christened as "improvement". It is a package to put the economy back on the rails by reviving planning and economic co-ordination between sectors, enabling efficient allocation of resources. A reduction in the rate of investment coupled with a reversal of the investment priorities ensured the consistency between growth of agriculture, light and heavy industry, between the means of production and means of consumption, and between accumulation and consumption. This period also witnessed

> a greater decentralization of power within the commune organization. The production teams, the lowest of the three tiers in the set up, became the basic accounting unit, which is the level at which the income generated in the commune is distributed. It paved the way for decentralization of economic power. The production teams also introduced material incentive for production, which were withdrawn during the Great Leap Forward. The agricultural policies were focused on agriculturally advanced and productive areas, that is the areas with high and stable yields. These brought some element of success into economic management and ensured balanced sectoral growth; agricultural and industrial output in 1963-65 increased by 15.7 percent per year and national income by 14.5 percent per year.

That an optimal share of accumulation in national income is essential for steady state growth can be observed from its association with the growth of the macro economic variables given in Table 1.4. The course of accumulation rate in 1952-78 shows the following:

(a) The production growth is relatively faster when accumulation rate ranges from 22 percent to 25 percent.
(b) The impediments to a reasonable standard of living surface as accumulation rate exceeds 30 percent.
(c) As accumulation rate surpasses 35 percent, the inter-sectoral balance of the economy gets distorted and the process of economic development suffers a setback.

The correlation coefficient between growth of macro-economic aggregates and accumulation rate is presented in the form of a matrix in Table 1.5. The rate of economic growth is strongly influenced by the relative rates of consumption and accumulation. There is a strong association between growth of national income and accumulation rate. Industrial growth, but not agricultural growth, is influenced by changes in accumulation rate.

Table 1.4: Growth and Accumulation Rate

(Per cent per year)

Period	*Accum-ulation Rate (percent)*	*Labour Productivity*	*National Income*	*Agriculture*	*Industry*
1. First Plan	24.8	8.7	8.9	4.5	18.0
2. Second Plan	31.6	–5.4	–3.1	–4.3	3.8
3. 1963-65	22.8	23.1	14.5	11.1	17.9
4. Third Plan	25.5	2.5	8.4	3.9	11.7
5. Fourth Plan	32.0	1.3	5.6	4.0	9.1

Note: 1. Labour productivity is measured for industrial enterprises under public ownership system.
2. The growth rates of agriculture and industry relate to value of output.

Source: Pei Yuanxiu, Liu Bingying and Li Bingzhong, *Guangming Ribao,* 26 June, 1980, p. 4, Beijing.

Table 1.5: Growth of Macro Variables: Correlation Matrix

	NT	*NA*	*NI*	*TC*	*RC*	*UC*	*RA*
NT	1.00	0.28	0.91	0.49	0.20	0.47	0.79
NA		1.00	0.05	0.83	0.86	0.54	0.19
NI			1.00	0.29	0.03	0.31	0.67
TC				1.00	0.85	0.75	0.29
RC					1.00	0.35	–0.01
UC						1.00	0.46
RA							1.00

Note: NT, NA and NI are national income total, from agriculture and from industry respectively and TC, RC and RU are total, rural and urban consumption respectively, expressed as yearly growth in real terms for the period 1952-78. RA is rate of accumulation.

The high correlation coefficient between growth of national income and industry (0.91) at the backdrop of low correlation between growth of national income and agriculture (0.28) is indicative of the bias towards industry. Private consumption is moderately influenced by income growth, perhaps due to alienation of the main stream of consumption from the market system, which was total by mid-1950s. The high correlation coefficient between agricultural growth and rural consumption (0.86) underlines the dependence of rural population on agriculture *per se.* The low correlation between accumulation rate and agricultural growth (0.19) merely attests that agriculture scarcely benefited from the growth process. The association between agricultural growth and urban consumption (0.54) reflect the dependence of urban population on supply of essentials from agriculture. The scenario symbolises a pure and simple model of extracting surplus from agriculture for industrial development.

The Reasons and Fall Out

The rise in accumulation rate was prompted by the emphasis on heavy industry. The share of heavy industry in total investment rose from 29.5 percent in 1952 to 50.9 percent in 1978. In tandem, the composition of output in 1952-78 witnessed a shift from agriculture to industry and also from light to heavy industry as can be observed from the sectoral composition of output, given in Table 1.6.

Table 1.6: Sectoral Composition of Output

(Percentage at current prices)

Sector	*1952*	*1957*	*1978*
1. Agriculture	56.9	43.3	27.8
2. Industry	43.1	56.7	72.2
2a. Heavy Industry	15.3	25.5	41.1
2b. Light Industry	27.8	31.2	31.1

Source: 1. *Economy,* The China Handbook Editorial Committee, Foreign Languages Press, Beijing, 1984, p. 49.
2. Table 1, p. 150, "Set Up of Production", by Sun Shangqing and Chen Shengchang in *China's Socialist Modernisation* (ed.) Yu Guangyuan, Foreign Languages Press, Beijing, 1984.

Average sectoral investment given in Table 1.7 show that three-fourth of the investment in agriculture and industry was for heavy industry. This distinct bias of investment in favour of heavy industry generated a growth profile, which is not inter-sectorally consistent.

Table 1.7: Average Investment and Output in 1952-78

Sector	*Investment Share (1952-78 average, per cent)*	*Output Growth (per cent per year)*
1. Agriculture	12.0	4.3
2. Light Industry	5.4	8.4
3. Heavy Industry	54.2	12.2
Total	71.6	7.7

Source: Ma Hong, *New Strategy for China's Economy*, New World Press, Beijing, 1983, p. 40.

Table 1.8: Capital Construction and Productive Accumulation

(*percentage*)

No.	*Period*	*Share of Capital Construction in Total Financial Expenditure*	*Share of Productive Sectors in Total Accumulation*
1.	First Plan (1953-57)	37.0	56.5
2.	Second Plan (1958-62)	46.2	86.7
3.	1963-65	-	65.9
4.	Third Plan (1966-70)	40.2	74.6
5.	Fourth Plan (1971-75)	40.7	75.3

Source: 1. *Statistical Yearbook of China*, State Statistical Bureau, Beijing, 1986, p. 54.

2. Ma Hong, *New Strategy for China's Economy*, New World Press, Beijing, 1983, p. 39.

Table 1.8 gives the share of capital construction in total financial expenditure and the share of productive sectors in total accumulation. The share of capital construction in total financial expenditure is high; more than 40 percent in the second, third and fourth plans, spanning over the period 1958 to 1970.

The inadequacy of investment in light industry adversely affected the production of consumer goods in general and wage goods in particular. The investment in housing was also inadequate and as a result, the average floor space in the cities reduced. A housing survey in 182 cities reveal a reduction in per person residential space from 4.5 square metres in 1952 to 3.6 square metres in 1978 and 37 percent of the households in cities were without adequate housing.[7]

A scheme was formulated at the beginning of the Second Plan to promote light industry. Subsequently, in 1958, a treatise on simultaneous development of large, medium and small enterprises and the concept of "five small-scale industries" was promoted. It covers iron and steel, hydro electricity, fertiliser, cement and kilns, all at a small scale such that the provincial governments are able to finance the investment. These were not adequate to prevent lopsided industrial growth as heavy industry crowded agriculture and light industry out. Average investment for the period 1958 to 1978 is 76 percent in heavy industry and 24 percent in agro-based and light industry.[8] Investment in heavy industry was mainly concentrated in metallurgical and machine building. Agriculture and light industry were inadequately assisted by heavy industry. In 1978, 29 percent of steel flowed to machine building, 15.3 percent to agriculture including maintenance and repair of agricultural machinery and 11.7 percent to light industry.[9]

Impact on Income and Wages

The prevalence of high accumulation rate yielded an income and output structure, which was not conducive to improvement in the standard of living of a vast majority of the population. The average income in rural and urban areas, given in Table 1.9 indicates a slow down of the growth rate in per capita rural income from 3.25 percent per annum in 1957-65 to 2.90 percent per annum in 1957-78. The slowdown is also observed in urban areas.

The real wages of workers and staff in urban areas began declining from 1957, even considering that income accrues not only from money wage but also from social benefits such as, free medical care, state subsidy for rent, water and electricity. These social benefits amounted to 14 percent of total wage, on the average in 1978.[10] The growth in average wage of staff and workers in state owned enterprises given in Table 1.10 shows that real wages declined in three of the five Five-Year Plans implemented in 1953-80. Even money wage or nominal wage declined in two Five-Year Plans.

Table 1.9: Urban and Rural Income

(Yuan, per capita, yearly)

Area	*1957*	*1965*	*1976*	*1978*
1. Rural	40.5	52.3	62.8	73.9
		(3.25)	(2.34)	(2.90)
2. Urban	637	652	605	644
		(0.29)	(–0.27)	(0.05)

Notes: 1. Rural income is denoted by commune salary and urban income by wages of workers and staff.

2. The figures in parentheses indicate annual average growth rates from 1957.

Source: Ma Hong, *New Strategy for China's Economy,* New World Press, Beijing, 1983, pp. 16-17.

Table 1.10: Growth of Wages in State Enterprises

(percent per year)

Period	*Money Wage*	*Real Wage*
1. First Plan (1953-57)	7.4	5.4
2. Second Plan (1958-62)	–1.5	–5.4
3. 1963-65	3.3	7.2
4. Third Plan (1966-70)	–1.4	–1.2
5. Fourth Plan (1971-75)	0.1	–0.1
6. Fifth Plan (1976-80)	5.5	2.9

Source: Xu Jiewen, *Jingji Yanjiu,* No. 11, 20 November 1985, pp. 52-65.

The reasons behind the decline in wages may partly be traced to the employment and wage policy, which prescribes a trade-off between increase in average wages of existing workers and staff and expansion of employment. The growth in work force demanded an additional four to five million jobs annually in urban areas. The allocation for wages in the state plan was utilised to increase employment opportunity *i.e.*, to meet wages of the newly employed and to raise wages of existing staff. Between 1953 and 1978, 56 percent of the increased allocation of wage in state units was earmarked to accommodate new employees and 44 percent for raising the wages of existing workers and staff.[11]

V
Personal Consumption

"The consumption pattern is not only determined by the state of development but also by the culture, habit, social system and the national situation."[12] This broadly explains the planners' attitude towards the standard of consumption that people at large were to enjoy under central planning.

The trend rate of growth of per capita consumption in 1952-78 is 1.9 percent per year in rural areas, 2.6 percent per year in urban areas and 2.0 percent per year for the country as a whole. The same in 28 low-income developing countries (those with per capita annual income of US $ 370 or less in 1979) for which data were available is estimated as 3.7 percent per year in 1960-79.[13] Average urban consumption, which was two and a half times of that in rural in 1952, widened to three times in 1978. This disparity was even more in economically distressing years.

The cost of living in the developing countries, which generally is higher in urban areas as compared to the countryside, is also evidenced in China. In 1952-78, retail prices rose by 22 percent as against 25 percent in cost of living of staff and workers in urban areas. The peasants had to sell a portion of the output to the state and/or in the market. The quantity sold to the state and the market as percentage to self-consumption is called the commodity rate and the products, which is so sold, is known as commodity item. These are mostly agriculture-based commodities and produced in the rural areas. The state used to requisition these items directly from the producers for distribution. The rise in the commodity prices caused decline in the per capita real consumption of those who were net buyers of these items. Much of the decline in the per capita real consumption in 1957-60 and also in 1965-76 was due to the rise in commodity prices.[14] In rural areas, per capita foodgrain consumption in 1978 was 5 percent less than in 1957, and that of edible oil, beef and mutton was two-third. Domestic production of basic necessities dipped so low that foodgrain, edible oil and sugar had to be imported in order to meet even this meagre consumption. The slide in the average consumption was slow but consistent from 1957 indicating that the economy failed to gain momentum after initial restoration following liberation.

The quantity of foodgrain available for consumption has been estimated as 390.92 jin (195.46 kilogram) per capita per year in 1978. It includes potato, corn, millet and other grains besides rice and wheat. In order to derive the estimate of consumption, 10 to 15 percent of the availability of rice and wheat has to be netted out as processing loss. Since the share of rice and wheat is about half of the total foodgrain availability, the per capita foodgrain consumption works out to less than 15 kilograms per month or about 500 grams per day. This is 80 percent of the requirement. The actual consumption of other food items such as oil, sugar, meat, fish and egg was 34 to 40 percent of the requirement.[15] It is obvious that the growth process was unable to generate sufficient wage goods. Even the domestic use of power remained in a rather crude form as 68.1 percent of fuel consumption was self-produced. By 1978, 87 percent of the communes, 62 percent of the production brigades and 50 percent of the production teams were connected with electricity. But, 70 percent of rural energy consumption came from bio-mass.[16]

The state monopoly in the marketing of essential items of consumption adversely affected both its quantity and quality. The state purchase of basic necessities, which includes the commodity items, on requisition basis or by assigning quota adversely affected production and in turn domestic supply. The supply system, which is the practice of providing basic necessities of life, free of charges, to those engaged in the liberation war, became a constraint in the improvement of consumption standard. It was an obligation, which the state took upon itself to repay some of the debts to those who made the idea of the People's Republic a reality. This could be implemented through a full-fledged rationing of the items of basic necessities. The ration system never allowed consumers to go by their tastes and preferences and restricted the choice of consumption basket. From the mid-1950s, the distribution of foodgrain and other consumer goods were channelised through coupons, which could be national, regional or departmental. The distribution of essential items through coupons can play a positive role under supply constraint. But it restricts consumer choice when effective demand is close to supply. In a country, where people owned the means of production, had very little say as consumers.

VI
A Stagnant Economy

The economy gathered considerable momentum during the initial period of restoration following the liberation. From 1949 to 1952, the country made great strides from economic prostration to growth. The first five-year plan (1953-57) is regarded as having been enormously successful as it was able to lay the foundation of heavy industry with the setting up of a number of industries in the area of cement, coal, iron and steel, electricity, machine building, etc. along with several thousands of smaller industrial and mining enterprises. The macro-economic indicators of growth and level of living emerged strongly. The table turned from 1958 with the Great Leap Forward, and the birth of the commune organisation.

Table 1.11: Investment Coefficient and Capital-Output Ratio

Sl. No.	*Period*	*Investment Coefficient*	*Capital-Output Ratio*
1.	First Plan (1953-57)	83.7	1.68
2.	Second Plan (1958-62)	71.4	—
3.	Third Plan (1966-70)	59.5	—
4.	Fourth Plan (1971-75)	61.4	3.76

Source: Ma Hong, *New Strategy for China's Economy*, New World Press, Beijing, 1983, pp. 20, 21 and 78.

The growth rates of agricultural and industrial output as well as national income until 1978 are less than that until 1957. The investment coefficient and capital-output ratio in different plan periods are given in Table 1.11. These show that the slow down of the growth rate is accompanied by decline in the investment coefficient and rise in the capital-output ratio. The investment coefficient, which represents the rate at which investment is generated into fixed assets, declined from 71.4 percent in the second plan to 61.4 percent in the fourth plan. This clear 10 percent point drop in the investment coefficient in a decade and a half is mainly attributable to the excessive inventory holding of the industrial enterprises caused by the production of sub-standard goods for which there was no market demand under normal circumstances. The capital-output ratio, which represents the investment requirement for unit increase in national income, rose from 1.68 in the first plan to 3.76 in the fourth plan. This doubling of the capital-output ratio in nearly two decades underlines the low efficiency in the capital utilization. It also tells the untold story of the failure of a large number of projects.

Table 1.12 gives the efficiency indicators of the state enterprises. Between 1957 and 1976, the efficiency indicators of state enterprises declined as: (a) profit as a percentage of fixed assets from 23.6 percent to 12.1 percent, (b) profit-output ratio from 24.7 percent to 13.5 percent and (c) ratio of profit and tax to investment from 34.7 percent to 19.3 percent. The share of circulating fund to output rose. These are partly due to the managerial inefficiency, but the fundamental reason is that the target growth rates were not derived from material balances in key areas and were not inter-sectorally consistent.

Table 1.12: Efficiency Indicators in State Enterprises

(percentage)

No.	*Indicator*	*1957*	*1976*
1.	Profit to Output	24.7	13.5
2.	Profit and Tax to Investment	34.7	19.3
3.	Profit to Fixed Asset	23.6	12.1
4.	Circulating Fund to Output	27.4	38.5

Source: Same as in Table 1.11

Considerable inter-regional and inter-personal inequality in the distribution of income and consumption accompanied this modest rate of economic growth realized in 1952-78. The inequality in per capita income is more than that in per capita consumption, which, in turn, is more than that in per capita foodgrain consumption. The mechanism of food distribution, which in urban areas was rationed and in rural areas was based on work point, was not able to wipe out the inequality in food consumption. It only prevented food consumption from falling below a minimum where people are threatened with acute hunger and malnutrition, except in unusually bad years. It is, however, no mean an achievement because, many developing countries, with similar per capita income were not able to provide what China could, to its people at large.

Table 1.13: Decadal Growth Rates of Macro Variables

(percent per year)

No.	*Period*	*Foodgrain Production*	*National Income*	*Per Capita Consumption*		
				Rural	*Urban*	*Total*
1.	1952-62	0.00	4.39	0.00	5.08	1.43
2.	1953-63	-1.39	2.44	0.00	3.49	0.00
3.	1954-64	0.00	0.00	0.00	3.55	0.00
4.	1955-65	0.00	0.00	0.00	3.74	1.41
5.	1956-66	0.00	0.00	2.13	3.76	2.29
6.	1957-67	1.73	0.00	3.77	4.21	3.45
7.	1958-68	2.84	0.00	5.24	4.79	4.52
8.	1959-69	4.06	3.26	6.90	5.29	5.74
9.	1960-70	4.94	5.88	7.33	6.46	6.52
10.	1961-71	4.76	8.39	6.94	7.14	6.61
11.	1962-72	4.06	8.69	6.05	6.89	6.01
12.	1963-73	3.79	8.22	5.51	5.95	5.45
13.	1964-74	3.56	7.46	4.97	5.25	4.99
14.	1965-75	3.59	7.07	4.38	5.29	4.56
15.	1966-76	3.46	6.67	4.02	5.52	4.38
16.	1967-77	3.45	6.89	3.70	5.75	4.24
17.	1968-78	3.62	6.71	3.64	6.09	4.32
18.	1969-79	3.65	5.79	3.45	6.45	4.32
19.	1970-80	3.15	5.32	3.60	6.90	4.59
20.	1971-81	3.03	5.51	4.21	7.19	5.08
21.	1972-82	3.26	5.87	4.89	7.25	5.54
22.	1973-83	3.36	6.22	5.45	7.90	6.05

Notes 1. The growth rates are estimated from exponential time trend equation.
2. Zero indicate absence of statistically significant rising or falling trend.

There were successes in other areas, which are as important to the quality of life as income or consumption. Adequate attention and care to health and sanitation freed the country from epidemics and improved the main socio-economic indicators considerably. Notable is the improvement in life expectancy, which at the national level nearly doubled between 1949 and the early 1980s. There are country and region specific evidences of co-existence of low level of socio-economic indicators and high income, and *vice versa*. The sustainability of the high socio-economic indicators have particularly been questioned in the absence of a minimum rate of income growth, suggesting that the progress in terms of the socio-economic indicators can not be equated directly with the material progress of a nation measured by the overall rate of income growth or the performance of the economy.

The performance of the economy can be assessed from the movement of the growth rate of macro economic variable such as, national income and private consumption, and also of the foodgrain consumption, a welfare indicator in China. The trend growth rates of these variables estimated for each decadal period from 1952 (using exponential time trend) show that the growth rates of : (a) national income declined initially but picked up only to be followed by a decline, (b) food production followed a similar pattern, but experienced more oscillation, (c) per capita consumption in rural areas encountered three clear cycles and (d) per capita consumption in urban areas had two distinct phases; it experienced a rising trend after a brief decline in the early 1960s. Table 1.13 gives the decadal growth rates.

Table 1.14: Linear Time Trend of Growth Rates

No	*Dependent Variable*	*Constant*	*Regression Coefficient*	*R-Bar Square*	*F-Value*
A.	1952-78				
	Foodgrain Production	0.622 (1.0)	0.1788 (3.85)	0.40	14.8
	National Income	1.420 (1.3)	0.2906 (3.56)	0.36	12.7
	Per Capita Total Consumption	1.919 (2.8)	0.1948 (3.79)	0.39	14.4
	Per Capita Rural Consumption	2.012 (2.2)	0.1657 (2.41)	0.19	5.8
	Per Capita Urban Consumption	3.729 (10.7)	0.1657 (6.24)	0.64	39.0
B	1961-78				
	Foodgrain Production	4.226 (25.6)	-0.0901 (4.33)	0.60	18.8
	National Income	8.635 (30.0)	-0.2577 (7.10)	0.80	50.4
	Per Capita Total Consumption	5.431 (11.6)	-0.0491 (0.83)	-0.03	0.7
	Per Capita Rural Consumption	5.689 (10.1)	-0.1444 (2.04)	0.21	4.2
	Per Capita Urban Consumption	5.692 (12.4)	0.1053 (1.83)	0.16	3.3

Notes: 1. Dependent variable is decadal growth rate of the variable.
2. The figures in the parentheses contain t-values.

Table 1.14 gives the linear time trend of the abovementioned trend growth rates. These linear trend equations can be used to test acceleration, deceleration or stagnancy of the growth rates. A positive and statistically significant regression coefficient of the linear time trend indicates acceleration in growth rate, while a negative and statistically significant regression coefficient indicates a deceleration. The growth rate is considered to have stagnated if the regression coefficient does not turn out to be statistically significant.

The linear time trend of decadal growth rates during the period 1952-78 demonstrate: (a) acceleration in the growth rate of per capita urban consumption, and (b) stagnancy in the growth rate of foodgrain production, national income and per capita rural consumption.

The performance of the growth rates is also assessed for the period 1961-78, i.e. excluding the early years of high growth (1952-57) and the economically distressing years (1958-60). The linear time trend of decadal growth rates in 1961-78 demonstrate (a) strong deceleration in the growth rates of national income and foodgrain production, and (b) stagnation in the growth rates of per capita consumption in rural and urban areas.

The strong deceleration in the growth rates of macro aggregates after 1961 is an eloquent testimony of the failure of central planning. The economic scenario in 1978 presents a candid litany of economic woes, which ultimately forced reconsideration of the planning and development strategy based on central planning. Indeed, the process of rolling back the frontiers of state intervention initiated at this time through economic reforms is an attempt to reformulate the planning and development strategy to return from the *cul-de-sac.*

REFERENCES

1. Kan Lun, *Guoji Maoyi Wenti,* No. 4, July-August, 1984, pp. 1-7, and No. 9, 27 September 1984, pp. 3-5, Beijing.
2. Lin-Hai-Yun, *Shih-Chich Chih-Shih,* No. 18, 20 September 1959; Wang Linsheng and Chen Yujie, "Economic Relations with Foreign Countries", in *China's Socialist Modernisation* (ed) by Yu Guangyuan, Foreign Languages Press, Beijing, 1984, p. 681.
3. Xu Dixin, *China's Search for Economic Growth,* Beijing, 1982, p. 167.
4. Article 15, *The Chinese Constitution,* Foreign Languages Press, Beijing, 1957.
5. *Ten Great Years,* Foreign Languages Press, Beijing, 1960, p. 47.
6. Walker, Keneth R., "Grain Self-Sufficiency in North China". *China Quarterly,* Vol. 71, 1977, quoted in Carl Riskin, "Feeding China:The Experience since 1949", in Jean Dreze, Amartya Sen and Athar Hussain (eds), *Political Economy of Hunger: Selected Essays,* Oxford University Press, 1995, p. 414; Dreze, Jean and Sen, Amartya, *India, Economic Development and Social Opportunity,* Oxford University Press, Third Impression, 1997, p. 75; Peng, Xizhe, "Demographic Consequences of the Great Leap Forward", *Population and Development Review,* Vol. 13, 1987; Ashton, B., Hill, K., Piazza, A. and Zeitz. R., "Famine in China, 1958-61", *Population and Development Review,* Vol. 10, 1984.
7. Dong Fureng, "Relationship between Accumulation and Consumption", in Xu Dixin. *Chinese Search for Economic Growth,* New World Press, Beijing. 1982.
8. Xia Zhen, "Guidelines Old and New", Economic Adjustment and Reform, *Beijing Review,* Beijing, p. 16, 1982.
9. Wu Jiang, *Red Flag,* in Chinese, No. 12, 16 June 1980, pp. 2-18, Beijing.
10. Ma Hong, *New Strategy for China's Economy,* New World Press, Beijing, 1983, pp. 16 and 24.
11. Xian Qiyuan, "Income Distribution", quoted in Xu Dixin, p. 115. *op. cit.*
12. *Red Flag,* in Chinese, No. 14, 16 July 1981, pp. 10-18.
13. *World Development Report,* 1981, Table 4, p. 140, The World Bank, Washington D.C., August 1981.
14. Lin Senmu and Zhou Shulian, *Red Flag,* in Chinese, No. 3, 1 February 1981, pp. 9-13.
15. Yan Ruizhen, *Jingji Yanjiu,* No. 7, 20 July, 1985, pp. 40-45.
16. *Renmin Ribao,* 17 March 1980, p. 3; Li Baihang, *Kunming Jingji Wenti Tansuo,* No. 8, 20 August 1984, pp. 30-33; Yang Jike, *Guangming Ribao,* 9 December 1982; Weng Yongxi, Wang Zhishan, Huang Jiangnan and Zhu Jiaming, *Jingji Yanjiu,* No. 11, 20 March 1981, pp. 12-13, Beijing.

2

Agriculture

Agriculture as in the low income developing economies shaped the pace of economic growth and became the source of livelihood for a majority of the population in China. Agriculture in China accounts for three-fifth of national income. Four-fifth of the population depends on agriculture for their livelihood, directly or indirectly. It played a critical role in the development process not only by way of income and employment generation but also by providing the surplus for industrial development.

I
Land and Infrastructure

China's large area does not endow its agriculture with a favourable land-man ratio. Its topography and climate are such that only 10.4 percent of the total land area is arable. Over time, per person availability of arable land reduced due to diversion of land from agriculture to non-agriculture and increase in agricultural labour force. Capital construction, irrigation systems, construction of roads, housing in the countryside and upcoming small cities encroached on agricultural lands. The decline in arable land was faster in fertile regions along the coast and eastern plains. Agricultural labour force increased by 120 million in 1952-78. Per capita availability of agricultural land reduced from 2.59 mu (0.173 hectare) in 1957 to 1.45 mu (0.097 hectare) in 1978 that is by 44 percent during this period. China's arable land per farm population in 1978 was about one-fourth of the average of its neighbouring countries and one of the lowest in the world.

The arable lands are grouped into three grades as high, medium and low yield according to their yield of output. Medium and low yield accounted for two-third of the total acreage while high yield accounted for the remaining one-third. In 1978, 48 percent of arable land was irrigated and it generated two-third of food output. Agricultural mechanisation could not keep pace with time as 70 percent of farm machinery was widely believed to be at least a quarter century of age and out of date. Agriculture used 13 percent of electricity generation in 1979.[1]

Land Reform

Based on the size of landholding and family income from all sources, the administration (of the People's Republic) classified the rural families into four groups as landlords, rich peasants, middle peasants and poor peasants. The classification of rural families into these four groups was complete by 1950. It yielded an extremely skewed distribution of land holdings, which nevertheless was a known fact. The pattern of land distribution was so skewed that landlords and rich peasants constituted 10 percent of the population and owned 70 percent of cultivated land. The middle and the poor peasants owned the remaining 30 percent of the land. Many of the middle peasants owned small or marginal holdings. The poor peasants were generally landless and worked as agricultural labourers. A few of them owned small or marginal holdings and they also had to work as agricultural labourers to supplement their income. The middle peasants generally did not have to work as agricultural labourers.

An equitable distribution of land, considered essential for agricultural growth and income generation for rural poor, received topmost priority after liberation. The Agrarian Reforms Law was promulgated in June, 1950 in order to introduce a peasant proprietorship by redistributing land. It gave poor peasants the necessary access to land. The middle peasants retained their existing holdings if it did not exceed the cut-off level set by reform quota. The rich peasants were allowed to retain that portion of land, which they used to cultivate either themselves or by hired labour. The portion they used to rent out was taken away.[2] In fact, the idea at this time was centered on ensuring equity in the distribution of land keeping the private ownership. The idea of collectivisation was not in the picture then. It came later.

The reform measures drastically transformed the land ownership pattern by distributing 46.6 million hectares of land to 300 million peasants. Per capita cultivated land at the time of liberation was about one-fifth of a hectare across the country. The reform measures yielded an average 2.4 mu (0.16 hectare) to poor peasants. 3.0 mu (0.20 hectare) to middle peasants, 3.82 mu (0.25 hectare) to rich peasants and 2.12 mu (0.14 hectare) to landlords.[3]

The land reform transformed the agrarian structure and its impact was clearly visible on agricultural production. Agricultural output in the First Plan, during which the land reform was implemented, increased substantially by 3.5 to 4 percent a year even without state investment. Obviously, the growth came from efficiency gains arising from land reform. However, the land holdings of the poor peasants and some of the middle peasants were too small to be economically viable. The subsistence nature of the small-scale peasant economy compelled them to sell their lands to big farmers and a polarisation of the rich and the poor was witnessed in rural areas, giving rise to tenant farming. By 1953 one in every ten households in Hubei, Hunan, Zhejiang and Guangdong turned creditor.[4] There were evidences of widespread usury. These gave birth to a neo-rich peasant class.

The State acted swiftly and assisted the peasants to organise Mutual Aid Team (MAT) in order to raise capital. By 1954, three-fifth of the peasants were incorporated into MATs, where they retained private ownership of land and other assets. This followed the collectivisation movement with the formation of elementary (also called lower stage) agricultural producers cooperatives, where peasants while retaining private ownership of land, pooled it for cultivation and distributed the income in proportion to both land and labour. By 1956, 96 percent of the peasant households were attached to elementary agricultural producers co-operatives. Among these, 87.8 percent were in advanced agricultural producers co-operatives, where land and other means of production such agricultural tools and implements, draught animals, etc. were collectively owned and income was distributed according to man-hours of work after necessary deductions on account of depreciation of means of production, state reserve and public welfare fund. The main difference between the elementary and the advanced stage producers co-operatives is that in the former the income was distributed mostly in proportion to the land owned by the family whereas in the latter, the distribution was made on the basis of the amount of labour put in by the family members. There were 740 thousand advanced agricultural producer co-operative societies in 1958. These were reorganised into 23,630 communes, which assumed the ownership of land and other agricultural assets of the peasants and made them its members in return.

II
Grain as a Key Link

The State shaped the agricultural policy by prescribing the cropping pattern, setting the price level and fixing the crop output targets. The strategy in agriculture placed a massive emphasis on foodgrain production, which was treated as the key link to ensure economic development. The philosophy was preached in full faith and the stress on foodgrain production became the hallmark of agricultural strategy.

Table 2.1: Foodgrain Output in Five-Year Plans

(billion jin)

Period	*Rice*	*Wheat*	*Others*	*Foodgrain*
1. First Plan (1953-57)	77.89	22.61	81.13	181.62
2. Second Plan (1958-62)	65.32	19.57	79.31	164.20
3. 1963-65	81.50	21.51	81.00	184.01
4. Third Plan (1966-70)	97.73	27.55	93.08	218.36
5. Fourth Plan (1971-75)	94.84	38.00	130.23	263.07
6. 1976-78	130.44	48.44	112.39	291.27

Notes: One billion jin is equivalent to half a million ton.
Source: China Agricultural Year Book, Beijing, 1982.

The production of major foodgrain in the Five-Year Plan periods is given in Table 2.1. The rate of growth of foodgrain production between the First (1953-57) and the Fourth (1971-75)

Plan is 2.08 percent per year. This being close to the population growth, implies stagnation in per capita foodgrain production between the First and the Fourth Plan (1953-75). The stagnation is due to low productivity in agriculture caused by the sole emphasis on foodgrain. Between 1965 and 1976, agricultural income rose by only 0.8 times whereas use of farm machinery and chemical fertiliser increased by 8.3 times and 2.6 times respectively.[5] Low farm prices resulted in low income of the peasants. Low farm income led to lower accumulation. Investment requirement in most of the communes was far greater than the accumulation, leading to stagnation in agricultural output and income. It was a vicious circle of low income and low investment. Diversification of agricultural activities through animal husbandry and agro-based industry are needed to break this vicious circle. The communes, which witnessed increase in incomes generally had a developed agri-business. The thrust on agricultural mechanisation took a back seat for twin reasons of paucity of investment and absence of alternative employment opportunity for the surplus manpower in agriculture. The fate of agriculture was linked to the state of the commune. The regions with weak infrastructure remained poor, as they were not allowed to embark on alternative activity before meeting their target of foodgrain production. The commune had to engage an army of under-employed in agriculture, which was the primary occupation of its members since production of foodgrain was the single most important factor. The search for self-sufficiency under unitary emphasis on foodgrain production went on and on for three decades ignoring the comparative advantage of regions.

Table 2.2: Sources of Agricultural Output

(Percentage)

No.	*Item*	*1952*	*1957*	*1975*
1.	Farming	83.1	80.6	72.5
2.	Animal Husbandry	11.5	12.9	14.0
3.	Sideline Business	4.4	4.3	9.1
4.	Forestry	0.7	1.7	2.9
5.	Fishing	0.3	0.5	1.5
6.	Total	100.0	100.0	100.0

Note: The percentages are calculated from the value of gross output.

Source: *Economy*, The China Handbook Editorial Committee, Table 4.4, p. 214, Foreign Languages Press, Beijing, 1984.

The sources of agricultural output given in Table 2.2 indicate that the policy of grain as a key link was translated into crop farming. The share of farming in gross value of agricultural output declined from 83.1 percent in 1952 to 72.5 percent in 1975. The share of animal husbandry rose marginally, from 11.5 percent to 14 percent during the same period. The share of sideline occupation was only 9.1 percent in 1975. The emphasis on foodgrain production at the expense of cash crop resulted in unbalanced growth of agriculture and interdicted the growth of animal husbandry, forestry, fishing and the agri-business.

Foodgrain output increased by 36 percent between 1965 and 1976. It was accompanied by 54 percent rise in cost of production and 20 percent fall in output-labour ratio. The ratio of agricultural to non-agricultural population was 4.9:1 in 1952. It remained unchanged in 1978. The agriculture continued to be the prime occupation for rural labour force. The flow of work force from agriculture to non-agriculture was restricted initially to force down the rural wage rate. Migration from rural to urban areas and also between rural areas was statutorily prohibited. The peasants were firmly tied to their native soil through the mechanism of household registration, with the carrot of employment, which rarely was full time, and ration, which in most cases was less than the bare minimum for survival. The responsibility of the peasants was to produce food for themselves and provide raw material for industry. Alternative occupational venture was beyond their imagination. The state of agriculture left a direct bearing on the standard of living as it was the source of 95 percent of consumption on food and clothing.[6]

The facet of agriculture did not change as 85 percent of rural labour force was engaged in farming. There is a symbiotic relationship between agriculture and rural non-farm sectors through forward and backward linkages. Non-farm employment in rural sector can effectively reduce seasonal unemployment in agriculture and also the incidence of underemployment. The evidence of agriculture and industry complementing each other is witnessed in the developing countries. In India, for example, one percentage point rise in agricultural growth in the 1970s is found to be correlated with 0.5 percent point rise in industrial growth and 0.7 percent point in national income.[7] Agriculture-industry linkage in a developing economy can be established through rural expenditure on manufactures. Increase in agricultural output raises household and government income, which in turn, stimulate the demand for consumer goods. Although per capita rural income is lower than in urban, absolute size of the market of manufactured goods is larger in the former because of higher population base. Moreover, the rural folks spend so much of additional income on manufactures that increase in agricultural income generates substantial demand for industrial goods. Agricultural sector, this way is potentially the major source of effective demand for industrial output of low capital intensity, which being mostly in the form of wage goods can improve the standard of living in rural areas.

These permutations draw the contour of agricultural activities *vis-a-vis* the entire economy. The agriculture never gained momentum after the commune was established. It revolved around foodgrain production and its growth was constrained by high proportion of farmers in agricultural labour force. The slow growth of farm output coupled with low farm prices stagnated farm incomes. Agriculture contributed only modestly to overall economic growth, which itself was modest. Egalitarianism in the distribution of income within the basic accounting units, stringent regulation on non-farm activity of the farming population, prohibition of private foodgrain sale, restriction on internal trade and promotion of self-sufficiency in staple food in the communes are identified as prime factors behind reducing the agricultural growth rate to modest.

III
The Pattern of Agricultural Growth

Agricultural production in the central planning era (1952-78) can distinctly be divided into two phases as pre- (1952-57) and post-commune (1957-78). The growth in agricultural production in pre-commune era owes more to area expansion whereas in the commune regime it originated more from rise in yield rate.

The growth in area and production of agricultural commodities are given in Table 2.3. The area under major food and commercial crops expanded in the pre-commune era, but declined thereafter. The area under foodgrain declined in 1957-78 even as the area under rice and wheat, corn and tuber rose though slower than in 1952-57. The area under oil-bearing crops declined.

Table 2.3: Agricultural Commodities: Growth in Area and Production

(per cent per year)

Crop	*Area 1952-57*	*Area 1957-78*	*Area 1952-78*	*Production 1952-57*	*Production 1957-78*	*Production 1952-78*
1. Rice	2.58	0.31	0.74	4.87	2.20	2.70
2. Wheat	2.14	0.28	0.63	5.45	4.00	4.28
3. Corn	3.53	1.39	1.80	4.94	4.67	4.72
4. Soybean	1.77	-2.72	-1.87	1.09	-1.34	-0.88
5. Tuber	3.85	0.56	1.18	6.06	1.78	2.59
6. Foodgrain	1.51	-0.49	-0.11	3.54	2.15	2.41
7. Cotton	0.70	-0.81	-0.52	4.69	1.34	1.97
8. Peanuts	7.09	-1.71	-0.08	2.11	-0.37	0.10
9. Rapeseed	4.37	0.57	1.29	-0.96	3.60	2.71
10 Sesame	-2.27	-2.35	-2.34	-8.29	0.15	-1.53

Notes: Estimated from semi-log regression from the data in *Statistical Year Book of China*, State Statistical Bureau, Beijing, 1986, pp. 137, 143 and 148.

The production growth of agricultural commodities has been significant in 1952-57, *i.e.*, before the formation of the communes and is equally dismal thereafter. The growth in foodgrain production slowed down from 3.54 percent in 1952-57 to 2.15 percent in 1957-78. The latter being close to the rate of growth of population, imply stagnancy in per capita foodgrain production in the commune regime. The growth in the production of commercial crop was still less. The production scenario thus had two distinct phases as pre- and post-commune. The land reform gave a boost to agricultural production, both of food and commercial crops in pre-commune regime by way of area expansion and use of latent energies. The emphasis on food crop in commune regime acted as a binding constraint on growth of commercial crop. The authority of commune and the associated state intervention in agriculture are believed to be responsible for retardation in the growth of agricultural output after 1957.

The Nature of Production

The output growth of rice, wheat, corn, and also of foodgrain in the pre-commune era (1952-57) is contributed by both area and yield, whereas in case of oil-bearing crops, the output growth is exclusively due to increase in area. After 1957, the output growth of agricultural commodities became dependent on yield rate. In case of oil bearing crops, the area under cultivation declined and the yield rate increased. As a result of area expansion, the corn output increased in 1957-78. The increase in the area under corn as compared to rice or wheat is largely due to its higher productivity in unirrigated areas. The increase in the area under rice and wheat particularly for modern varieties, which requires assured water supply is constrained by irrigation facility. The production of rice and wheat was inadequate in relation to domestic demand and corn assumed a major share.

Rice and wheat, the two superior varieties of cereals are most preferred items in the consumption basket of the Chinese. Table 2.4 gives the area and production of rice and wheat and their share in foodgrain. The area under rice and wheat increased until 1957. These declined afterwards. It was in 1970 that the area under rice recovered its 1957 level. It took another five years for wheat to reach the same. Also, the share of rice and wheat together in foodgrain production remained stagnant in 1957-70. After 1970, the share of rice in foodgrain production remained stable while that of wheat increased. The increase in the share of wheat is exclusively attributed to growth in yield rate, which by all means is the offspring of modern variety. The relatively higher growth in yield of wheat is a global phenomenon, rather than an achievement that can exclusively be attributable to China. Although modern variety of wheat found its way into Asia by the early 1960s, the Chinese seems to lag behind in adapting it.

Table 2.4: Rice and Wheat in Foodgrain Production

No.	*Item*	*1952*	*1957*	*1970*	*1975*	*1978*
1	Area (million hectare)					
	a) Foodgrain	124.0	133.6	119.3	121.1	120.6
		(87.8)	(85.0)	(83.1)	(80.9)	(80.3)
	b) Rice	28.4	32.2	32.3	35.7	34.4
		(22.9)	(24.1)	(27.1)	(29.5)	(28.5)
	c) Wheat	24.8	27.5	25.5	27.7	29.2
		(20.0)	(20.6)	(21.4)	(22.8)	(24.2)
2	Production(million tonnes)					
	a) Foodgrain	163.9	195.0	240.0	284.5	304.8
	b) Rice	68.4	86.8	110.0	125.6	136.9
		(41.7)	(44.5)	(45.8)	(44.1)	(44.9)
	c) Wheat	18.1	23.6	29.2	45.3	53.8
		(11.1)	(12.1)	(12.2)	(15.9)	(17.7)
3	Yield(kilogram per hectare)					
	a) Foodgrain	1322	1460	2011	2349	2527
			(2.00)	(2.49)	(3.16)	(2.46)
						((2.90))
	b) Rice	2411	2692	3405	3517	3978
			(2.23)	(1.82)	(0.65)	(4.19)
						((1.96))
	c) Wheat	732	858	1145	1635	1845
			(3.23)	(2.24)	(7.38)	(4.11)
						((6.14))

Notes: 1. The figures in the parentheses of foodgrain given in 1(a) indicate percentage of area under foodgrain to total cultivated area.
2. The figures in the parentheses of rice and wheat given in 1(b) and 1(c) indicate their percentage shares in total area under foodgrain.
3. The figures in the parentheses of production of rice and wheat given in No. 2 indicate their percentage shares in total foodgrain production.
4. The figures in the single parentheses of yield rate given in No. 3 indicate annual average growth rates from the year mentioned in the preceding column. The figures in double parentheses indicate annual average growth for the period 1970-78.

Source: Estimated from the data in *Statistical Yearbook of China*, State Statistical Bureau, Beijing, 1986, pp. 137 and 143.

The diversification of agricultural production called for reduction in area under food crops and expansion of cash crop. Area shift from food to cash crop demands productivity growth of food crops. The composition of area and production for food crops in

1952 and 1978 given in Table 2.5 is an appraisal of the damages inflicted on agriculture. The increase in the share of major grains *viz.*, rice, wheat, corn, soybean and tuber, in the total sown area by 15.6 percent point from 1952 to 1978 was necessitated mainly due to the inability of the food producing sector to match the demand.

Table 2.5: Composition of Food Crops

(Percentage)

Crop	*Area 1952*	*Area 1978*	*Production 1952*	*Production 1978*
1. Rice	22.9	28.5	41.7	44.9
2. Wheat	20.0	24.2	11.1	17.7
3. Corn	10.1	16.6	10.3	18.4
4. Soybean	9.4	5.9	5.8	2.5
5. Tuber	7.0	9.8	10.0	10.4
6. Major Grains	69.4	85.0	78.9	93.9

Source: Same as in Table 2.3.

Between 1952 and 1978, the share of major grains in foodgrain production increased by 15 percent point; the share of rice, wheat and corn increased more, by 17.9 percent point. It underlines the dominance of cereal output in agriculture. This coupled with the agriculture as the prime occupation of a majority of the population present a classic case of economic backwardness that characterise a typical low-income developing country. Viewed from an alternative angle, a majority of the population in these countries are required and kept engaged in the production of basic necessities. Food being the major component of subsistence renders agriculture as the main productive occupation. Low labour productivity in such countries forces concentration of the work force in agriculture where cereal production tends to predominate because of its higher calorific value per unit of land as compared to non-cereal or animal products.

Sources of Output Growth

A quantitative assessment of the contribution of area and yield in the output growth of major items of foodgrain is made in Table 2.6. The estimates are made for the period 1952-78 and separately for pre- (1952-57) and post-commune (1957-78) period. From this, 59 percent of the increase in foodgrain output in 1952-57 came from increase in yield rate and 41 percent from area increase. The scenario is different in 1957-78 when the relative contribution of yield becomes more than area. The output growth of rice, wheat and corn, the three major food crops accounting for 80 percent of the foodgrain production, is almost exclusively due to increase in the yield rate as more than 79 percent of their increase in output came from rise in yield. The origin of output growth of major foodgrain items in the pre-commune era is traced from both area and yield, whereas in the commune era, it is traced almost exclusively to yield growth.

Table 2.6: Sources of Output Growth of Foodgrain

(Percentage)

Crop	*1952-57 Yield*	*1952-57 Area*	*1957-78 Yield*	*1957-78 Area*	*1952-78 Yield*	*1952-78 Area*
1. Rice	49.3	50.7	88.3	11.7	78.7	21.3
2. Wheat	63.3	36.7	95.3	4.7	91.0	9.0
3. Corn	30.5	69.5	79.1	20.9	74.6	25.4
4. Tuber	39.2	60.8	72.3	27.7	62.1	37.9
5. Foodgrain	59.0	41.0	117.3	–17.3	103.2	–3.2

Note: The impact of area and yield on production growth is estimated as:
Yield Impact = [(PT – AT × PO/AO)/(PT – PO)] × 100
Area Impact = [(AT × PO/AO – PO)/(PT – PO)] × 100

PO and PT are production in base and terminal year respectively and AO and AT are area in base and terminal year respectively.

Amplitude of Fluctuation

Foodgrain production exhibited a rising trend amidst severe annual fluctuation, mainly arising from its inability to cope with the aberrations of nature. The amplitude of fluctuation of foodgrain production can be measured from the coefficient of variation of residuals of the trend equation through which its annual growth rates are estimated. It can also be quantified by root mean absolute error, defined as the ratio between mean of absolute values of residuals of the trend equation and the mean of actual production. The amplitude of fluctuation of output has been estimated for foodgrain output and separately for rice and wheat, for the period 1952-78.

First, the trend growth rates of output of these items are computed from semi-log regression for the period 1952-78. These trend growth rates are found to be statistically significant Then, the amplitude of fluctuation of output for rice, wheat and foodgrain, measured by the coefficient of variation of the residuals are estimated as 75 percent, 81 percent and 64 percent respectively and by root mean absolute error as 8.6 percent, 12.1 percent and 8.2 percent respectively. Weather induced fluctuation in food output is observed to be large in relation to economically significant changes in the trend.

The nature of fluctuation of food output assessed from the correlation matrix of residuals indicates similarity in the fluctuations of rice and foodgrain. The correlation coefficient between the residuals of rice and foodgrain equation is high (0.84) but low (0.39) in case of wheat underlining the dissimilarity in their fluctuation. The fluctuation of rice and wheat is also not similar.

The Course of Foodgrain Production

The course of foodgrain production in a low-income developing country may be viewed in three phases. The first phase is to satisfy the minimum needs in terms of quantity, as elimination of starvation or semi-starvation is a matter of concern to the society. The second phase is to satisfy quality responses. The third phase is a gradual switch to non-cereal and non-grain food, mostly produced in animal husbandry and dairying sector. The indications are that China's state of foodgrain production in 1978 remained in the first phase.

Table 2.7: Growth of Foodgrain Output

(percent, per year)

No.	*Year*	*1952*	*1957*	*1978*
1.	1949	13.2	7.0	3.5
2.	1952	—	3.5	2.4
3.	1957	—	—	2.1

Notes: The periodicity of the growth rates relate to the year mentioned in the row to that in the column.

The growth of foodgrain output (which includes potato, corn, millet and other coarse grains besides rice and wheat), for different periods are given in Table 2.7. It shows that the initial spur following land reform was great by contemporary standards. Afterwards, the growth rate slowed down from 3.5 per cent per annum.... In 1952-57 to 2.4 percent per year in 1952-78 and further to 2.1 percent per year in 1957-78. A three-year average, to eliminate yearly fluctuation shows that per capita foodgrain consumption declined from 197 kilogram in 1952-54 to 192.5 kilogram in 1976-78. The extent and regional spread of foodgrain deficit is such that the dependence exceeded 150 percent in eight provinces.[8] Foodgrain production was neither balanced nor stable; it did not have even a reasonable capacity to withstand the aberrations of nature. However, it would be unfair to attribute the growth of agriculture as totally insignificant for its ability to prevent widespread hunger and starvation except in unusually bad years.

IV
Regional Issues

The strategy of agricultural development was not tailored to the regional needs and as a consequence, the output of agriculture and particularly of foodgrain was concentrated in the regions well endowed with infrastructure. It led to asymmetry in agricultural growth, which is evident from 15 percent of the counties generating 36 percent of foodgrain output and 49 percent of state purchase of foodgrain in 1978.[9] The south with 40 percent of arable land accounted for 58.4 percent of agricultural output in 1979 whereas per capita foodgrain production in certain areas of north-east Shanxi, north-west Shandong, eastern Henan, western Hubei, northern and southern Shaanxi, Yunnan, Guizhou and Ningxia remained well below the national average. The regional disparity in agricultural production could not be checked as investment flowed to areas with higher growth potential, a *la* the developed regions. The existence of low yield areas within the agriculturally developed regions characterise such uneven development. Examples are cited from Henan and Heilongjiang, though these are evident in other agriculturally developed regions also.

The process of agricultural development in Henan can be identified as an inter-mix of regions with extraordinary variation in yield. The yield of foodgrain in high, medium and low yield areas of Henan show that the difference between the maximum and the minimum yield of foodgrain is 25 percent in twenty two production brigades of high yielding areas, 46 percent in thirty four production brigades of intermediate yield and 61 percent in low yield areas.[10] The nature of productivity differential in agriculture is such that variation within low yield areas is more than that in medium yield areas, which again is more than that in high yield areas. Besides, there is variation in the yield rate of foodgrain within high, intermediate and low yield areas.

Table 2.8: Foodgrain Yield in Heilongjiang

(jin per mu)

Period	*Average*	*Minimum*	*Maximum*
1. First Plan (1953-57)	138 (1035)	114 (855) [1957]	187 (1403) [1955]
2. Second Plan (1958-62)	115 (863)	92 (690) [1960]	153 (1148) [1959]
3. Third Plan (1966-70)	192 (1440)	146 (1095) [1969]	231 (1733) [1967]
4. Fourth Plan (1971-75)	172 (1290)	120 (900) [1973]	223 (1673) [1975]
5. Fifth Plan (1976-80)	215 (1613)	197 (1478) [1977]	242 (1478) [1980]

Notes: The figures in ( ) are yield rates expressed as kilogram per hectare and in [ ] are the years in which the yield rate is realized.

Source: Zhong Chenglin, *Nongye Jishu Jingji*, No. 8, August, 1985, pp. 37-38.

The peak and trough in the yield rate of foodgrain within a five year plan period in Heilongjiang is an evidence of not only the existence of low yield areas within an agriculturally developed province but also its inability to withstand the aberrations of nature. The average yield of foodgrain with minimum and maximum in the First to Fifth Five Year Plan in Heilongjiang are given in Table 2.8. The average yield increased over the plan periods; and so also the difference between maximum and minimum yield within a Five-Year Plan. Two factors contributed to this widening of the difference between the maximum and the minimum within a Five-Year Plan period. First, application of modern technology increased the yield rate in a few areas. Second, yield rate declined sharply in years of natural calamity such as drought or flood.

The variation in climate and topography between warm and fertile regions of south and colder regions in north or between central inland and fertile eastern seaboard areas gave rise to regional imbalance in agricultural production, particularly of staple food. The average production in arid areas, constituting half of the total area under cultivation, was low and fluctuated widely due to dependence on weather. The risk and uncertainty of crop production in these areas led to concentration of agricultural investment in irrigated areas, which ensured higher productivity. Modern technology bypassed the arid areas, which characterise high risk, low investment, traditional technology and low production. The promotion of dry land agriculture got a back seat since the focus was on areas with higher growth potential. This acted as a catalyst in the widening of disparity in agricultural output and income between the developed and arid areas. The arid areas remained as some of the poorest and backward regions in the country.

The more unequal foodgrain production is between regions, the more is the inequality in its distribution. Transport constraint came in the way of smooth flow of foodgrain between deficit and surplus areas and proved extremely difficult to regulate supply in both bumper and lean years. Greater regional dispersal of food production could have alleviated the strain on transportation and storage and at the same stroke, diversified the food intake.

The regional inequality in foodgrain production caused imbalances in marketing, which can be seen from the output balance of rice, wheat and corn given in Table 2.9. At the national level, the production and demand in 1982 is such that there is deficiency of rice at the backdrop of surplus of wheat, corn and also of foodgrain. North and north-west are deficit in rice, wheat and corn. North-east is surplus in corn and deficit in rice. The provinces in Chang valley are surplus in wheat and face shortage of rice and corn. Similar is the production pattern in south, which is deficit in foodgrain. Southwest is surplus in rice and wheat and deficit in corn. Anhui, Henan and Jiangsu are foodgrain surplus, three-fourth of which is rice and wheat.

In the ultimate, the causes of these imbalances can be traced to the regional differential in land-water infrastructure and extension facility for regional agricultural systems. A strategy of crop diversification is essential to ensure optimal use of land and water and growth in gross cropped area. This besides maximizing the income and employment in agriculture can be effective in redressing the inter-crop imbalance.

Table 2.9: Regional Food Balance: 1982

(Billion jin)

Region	*Output*	*Total*	*Rice*	*Wheat*	*Corn*
1. North-East	74.34 (808)	+55	-60	+3	+115
2. North	116.52 (606)	–101	–74	–17	-9
3. An-He-Ji	143.91 (766)	+98	+41	+33	+3
4. Chang Valley	149.01 (789)	+39	–24	+86	–16
5. South	79.60 (634)	–24	–29	+10	–2
6. South-West	107.92 (655)	+8	+8	+12	-9
7. North-West	39.92 (568)	–17	–5	–3	–5
Total	711.22 (689)	+58	–143	+124	+77

Notes: 1. North-east includes Liaoning, Jilin and Heilongjiang; Beijing, Hebei, Tianjin, Shanxi and Inner Mongolia constitute the North; Chang Valley include Hubei, Hunan, Jiangxi, Zhejiang and Shanghai; Fujian, Guangxi and Guangdong constitute the south; Sichuan, Yunnan, Guizhou and Xinjiang constitute the south-west; North-west constitute Shanxi, Gansu, Ningxia and Qinghai.

2. In Sl. No. 3, An-He-Ji represent Anhui, Henan and Jiangsu.
3. The figures in brackets are per capita output, expressed as jin per year.
4. Last four columns give the balance, (+) denotes surplus and (–) deficit.
5. One billion jin is equivalent to half a million ton.

Source: Kuang Chanjuan and Xue Zhishi, *Nongye Jishu Jingji*, No. 5, May 1985.

Investment in agriculture declined and so also output-investment ratio. It implied a rise in the incremental capital-output ratio. The inadequacy of agricultural investment forced its channelisation into more productive regions and also to projects with short gestation lag and low capital intensity and thereby keeping the issue of regional dispersal of foodgrain production as distant as ever.

A broad-based policy of agricultural growth backed up by adequate infrastructure was essential for accelerating growth of agricultural output, reducing its amplitude of fluctuation and eliminating inter-regional and inter-crop disparity. The diversification of agriculture and diffusion of agricultural productivity demanded investment planning and project formulation based on intensive input-output studies. These could have provided the necessary impetus to rural development through dispersal of agro-industries and contributed more effectively to productivity and self-reliance. But, each region being indoctrinated with the fantasy of self-sufficiency, discarded comparative advantages and arranged their own comprehensive schemes of production. In an attempt to grow foodgrain first with whatever resource one had and then cogitating something else, agriculture continued to stagnate, accommodating an army of underemployed and ensnaring the rural economy into a low level equilibrium trap. The policy of grain as a key link neither enabled the agriculture to develop nor ensured all round development.

V
State Farm

The State Farm Bureau was set up in the early 1950s for diffusion of agricultural technology in the underdeveloped regions. About 4 percent of the total cultivated area in the country was under the state farms. The state farms are mainly located in the frontier areas or in the remote areas of the north-west. The provinces with considerable presence of the state farms are: Inner Mongolia, Heilongjiang, Liaoning, Guangdong, Fujian and Jilin. The state farms, as the name suggests, were state owned, headed by a state appointed Director and its employees received their wages from the state. The number of state farms increased from 562 in 1952 to 2067 in 1978. The expansion of the state farms in terms of investment, output and employment was phenomenal until the mid-1960s.

Activity Profile

Each state farm specialised in a particular activity, known as its principal activity, which was tailored to the local requirement. The principal activity profile of the state farms in 1978 was: 48 percent of the farms in foodgrain and cash crop, 21 percent in animal husbandry and dairying, 14 percent in fruits and tea plantation, 8 percent in rubber plantation and other tropical crop and 9 percent in medicinal herbs and miscellaneous activities. In 1980, 55.6 percent of the output in the state farms originated in agriculture and 44.4 percent in industry. Agricultural output comprised of 59.6 percent in crop farming, 13 percent in animal husbandry, 13.8 percent in rubber, 2.6 percent in forestry and 11 percent in sideline production.

Operational Efficiency

The output per unit of investment in fixed assets and profit per unit of investment and output can be used to measure the operational efficiency of the state farms. The provincial average and the maximum and the minimum of these indicators are given in Table 2.10.

Table 2.10: Efficiency Indicators in State Farms

(Percentage)

Ratio of	*Maximum*		*Minimum*		*Average*
1. Output to Investment	171.7	(300.0)	21.7	(10.0)	85.1
2. Profit to Investment	16.8	(100.0)	-3.9	(–80.0)	4.2
3. Profit to Output	16.2	(70.0)	–	(–300.0)	6.0
4. Labour Productivity (Yuan)	2310	(5500)	624	(200)	1859

Note: The figures in brackets are at farm level averages.

Source: 1. Luo Fu, *Beijing Review*, quoted in *Zhongguo Nongken*, No. 9, 24 September, 1980, p. 5.

2. Ding Lushu, *Zhongguo Nongken*, No. 10, 24 October 1980, pp. 7-10.

Inter-provincial variation of output to investment in the state farms is about eight times. The inter-farm differential is far more. The differential in case of average labour productivity, profit-investment ratio and profit-output ratio is similar.

The state of affairs in the state farms is primarily determined by the structure of the cost of production in agricultural and allied activities. Inter-farm variation in the cost of production is considerable in foodgrain, edible oil, meat and milk. The disparity is greater between production units within a farm. It is the direct outcome of differential productivity and operational efficiency.[11] In 1978, two-fifth of the state farms incurred loss. Even the industrial enterprises, which are generally considered profitable, do not portray a bright picture. One-third of the state farms specialised in industry were in the red. A study of 223 large-scale industrial enterprises in the late 1970s shows that 159 earned profit to the tune of 108.31 million Yuan whereas 64 incurred loss of 23.44 million Yuan.[12]

REFERENCES

1. *Renmin Ribao,* 17 March 1980, p. 3, Beijing.
2. *Agrarian Reforms Law of the People's Republic of China,* Foreign Languages Press, Beijing, Fourth Edition, 1953.
3. Liu Suinian and Wu Chungen (ed), *A Concise History of China's Socialist Economy,* Heilongjiang People's Publishing House, 1985, pp. 37-42.
4. Wang Songpei and Zhu Tiezhen, *Jingji Yanjiu,* No. 6, 20 June 1981, pp. 44-50.
5. Yan Zelong, *Guangming Ribao,* 21 September 1979, p. 2.
6. Liu Zhi Cheng, Zhou Wei and Huang Bufan, *Nongye Jishu Jingji,* No. 1, January 1984, pp. 1-6.
7. *World Development Report, 1986,* The World Bank and Oxford University Press, 1986, p. 80.
8. Yang Jun, *Nongye Jingji Wenti,* No. 8, 1980, Beijing.
9. Liang Yan, *Red Flag,* in Chinese No. 5, 1 March 1981, pp. 24-26.
10. Xiang Yang, *Guangming Ribao,* 9 June 1980, p. 2.
11. *Zhongguo Nongken,* No. 3, 24 March 1980, pp. 5-6 and No. 1, 24 January 1980, pp. 2-3, and pp. 6-8.
12. Ding Lushu, *Zhongguo Nongken,* No. 10, 24 October 1980, pp. 7-10.

3

The Commune and Rural Development

The Rural People's Commune was set up in 1958 in order to build the fabric of a self-sufficient rural economy while perpetuating the transition from collective to social ownership of the means of production. The communes integrated agriculture with industry and commerce and in the endeavour to secure the rural folks a higher standard of living, it became the focal point of rural development until economic reforms were initiated at the Third Plenary Session of the Eleventh Central Committee of the Chinese Communist Party in December 1978.

I
The Canopy

The collectivization movement in agriculture culminated in the formation of advanced agricultural cooperative societies throughout the rural areas of the country. Land and other means of production in these co-operative societies were collectively owned and incomes were distributed according to man-hours of work. By 1956, there were 740 thousand such societies in the rural areas of the country.

In August 1958, these advanced agricultural cooperative societies were reorganised into a three-tier ownership structure as: (a) the commune, (b) the production brigade, and (c) the production team. The economies of scale and administrative problems associated with the construction of large and medium scale projects (mostly irrigation projects) whose scope extended to more than one society are believed to be motivating factor behind this reorganization.

The basic data relating to the commune organisation are given in Table 3.1.

Table 3.1: Structure of Commune Organisation

No.	*Item*	*Unit*	*1958*	*1962*	*1978*
1.	Commune	Nos	23630	74771	52781
2.	Production Brigade	Thousand	-	703	690
3.	Production Team	Thousand	-	5580	4816
4.	Rural Households	Million	129	134	173
5.	Households per Commune	Nos	5459	1794	3287
6.	Households per Production Brigade	Nos	-	191	251
7.	Households per Production Team	Nos	-	24	36

Source: *Statistical Year Book of China*, State Statistical Bureau, Beijing, 1981, p. 133.

The Organisation and Management

The communes are divided into production brigades, which in terms of coverage of households and area, resemble the advanced agricultural co-operative societies. The production brigades are divided into production teams, which consists of about 30 families in an analogous area. The commune, without compensation requisitioned the assets of the peasants, which had been pooled into these agricultural co-operatives and made the peasants its members. The asset of the peasants this way was brought under state ownership and the income generated in communes was distributed among them in return.

The administrative and managerial functions of the commune were vested in a commune management committee, headed by a director and assisted by several deputy directors, who were elected by the commune members for a two-year tenure. The production brigade was administratively under the commune and had an elected management to overview the working of its industrial enterprises and undertakings. The production team was administered by a committee, which operated under the guidance of the commune and the production brigade.

The commune administration was fully bureaucratized and the state was the final authority in the formation of these committees.

Ironically, most of the administrative and managerial posts in the commune organization were occupied by the urbanites though it was a rural area organization and was to work for the rural people. The bureaucratic set-up in the commune organization was not at all different from the rural administrative structure found in most developing countries.

Team-Brigade-Commune Nexus

The major task of the commune is to integrate the plans of its production brigades and teams with the provincial plan. Agriculture is the major pre-occupation of the commune organisation and the responsibility is divided 'between the households and the three tiers, *i.e.*, production teams, brigades and commune, each with a specific role. The production team is directly responsible for organising production in the countryside and distribution of income. It also arranges the consumption requirements of its members. The production brigade co-ordinates the activities of production teams and carries out social service. The planning and development of agro-based industry is a major task of the production brigade. The nexus of the three tiers is focused on the form of ownership of the means of production, relation between various social groups and the State, and the manner of distribution of income among the members.

The communes enjoyed autonomy to the extent the State permitted inter-commune exchange of agricultural produce and commercial product. It also enjoyed the power to allocate (agricultural) input and credit and transfer of population from agriculture to non-agriculture such as in commune industry or in city. These powers were supposed to facilitate not only maximisation of income but also its equal distribution between production teams and brigades. The communes were empowered to transfer foodgrain from surplus to deficit areas to ensure equity in its consumption.

Though the area of governance of each of the three tiers of the commune organisation was statutorily set, the quadripartite division of responsibility between the households and the three tiers gave birth to a series of contradictions which came in the way of smooth implementation of the policies and programmes of the state plan.

These contradictions basically originated from the issues of autonomy of the basic accounting unit and the method of distribution of income, and were sought to be resolved from: (a) self-determination of the basic accounting unit to solve the conflict between the State and the collective economic unit, (b) democratic functioning at all levels of the commune organisation to remove the wrangling between officials and peasants and, (c) the principle of income distribution "to each one according to his work", so as to protect the individual interests.[1]

The area of conflict at the ground level was wide. The production team as the basic accounting unit earmarked the quantum of income for distribution among its members and was responsible for the overall financial performance. But their rights in respect of farming, production, management and distribution of produce were circumscribed by the guidelines of production brigade and commune. In order to iron out inter-production team disparity in per capita income, the relatively resourceful ones were often directed to undertake projects with the poorer ones, sharing equally the investment and material costs, regardless of the benefit accrued to them. Inter-production team exchange of manpower, particularly skilled manpower required approval of the commune and in some cases, of the state plan. The communes guided the production brigades and received instructions from the provincial administration. Each one spoke *ex-cathedra* and the underlined chain of dependency and authority permeating through the bureaucracy were similar to the administrative set-up in most developing countries. Moreover, all major decisions were draped in such imperial secrecy that could parallel only the operations of transnational corporations of the developed capitalist world.

The guidelines issued to the basic accounting units indeed aimed to promote equity with growth. But, in the environs of land quality dictating income inequality, the attempt to redistribute assets to eliminate income differential of the peasants impaired their activism. In the absence of personal incentive to acquire tangible wealth, the commune members became insensitive. The commune represented the classic case of the state becoming responsible for everything but in the end no one was responsible for the state.

II
The Basis of Distribution

The method of income distribution among the commune members attracted considerable attention for its role in ensuring equity in rural areas. The choice of the base of distribution *i.e.*, the basic accounting unit remained at the heart of this debate during the two decades (1958-1978) of the existence of the commune organisation.

Basic Accounting Unit

Basic accounting unit is the level at which financial accounting and distribution of collective income is made. Initially, it was the commune. The relatively richer production brigades and teams resented it, as they were forced to share their earnings with the poorer ones. The richer peasants already had a grudge as they bore most of the burnt of the State's decision to requisition the land and other agricultural assets with which the commune was formed. The State soothed their discontent by changing the basic accounting unit from commune to production brigade in February 1959. It replaced the averaging of poor and rich production brigades and teams within the commune by averaging of poor and rich teams within the brigade and narrowed down the area of dispute from the level of production brigade to production team. This arrangement was not favoured by the richer production teams within the brigade as they had to share their income with the poorer teams. It was not conducive to increase in agricultural production, as the richer teams within the brigade were responsible for a bigger share of output.

The fall in agricultural output associated with the Great Leap Forward forced the State to reconsider the base of accounting so as to provide adequate incentive to peasants, which seemed essential to raise production. The State, acting on a Draft Working Regulations of the Rural People's Communes (widely known as Sixty Articles) in 1961, made the production teams as the basic accounting unit in those production brigades where income and output was not exceptionally high. The production brigades remained as the basic accounting unit in the areas with exceptionally high income and output. It eliminated equal treatment of poor and rich production brigades in the distribution of income in non-rich areas. In areas with high income and output, the income of the relatively richer production teams within the brigade was at par with the poorer ones. The richer production teams in these areas continued to resent and wanted production team as the basic accounting unit. A compromise formula was evolved. The production brigades remained the basic accounting unit only after granting the production teams certain rights of ownership and managerial powers while contracting output targets from the brigade.

The choice of the basic accounting unit after the disastrous consequence of Great Leap Forward clearly recognised the association between personal incentive to earn more and agricultural production. It also set aside the idea of equity, as it was not possible to raise agricultural production by emphasising equality in the distribution of income, which in this context became synonymous with identical income irrespective of the labour productivity and contribution of factor input. The trade-off between growth and equity was tilted in favour of growth with the decision to transform production teams into basic accounting unit in February 1962. Production team as the basic accounting unit, needless to say, was unfavourable to the less well-endowed teams; also it had the seeds of increasing inter-personal income differential.

The supremacy of the production team in the area of production planning and income distribution can be said to have introduced the concept of grass-root planning. But, the committees that existed at commune and production brigade level greatly eroded the autonomy of the production teams and along with it, the features of grass-root planning.

Distribution of Income

The income in the communes is determined at the level of the basic accounting unit. The value of the produce in the basic accounting unit is termed as the gross income. The net income is obtained by deducting overhead and production expenses, investment fund and, conditions permitting, some grain for reserve, from gross income. The net income is distributed among the members of the basic accounting unit as wages. Setting the criterion for distribution is an onerous task.

The income of the basic accounting units is distributed on the basis of work point earned by the member. The calculation of work point varied inter-temporally and inter-regionally around two principal methods, based on: (a) fixed production quota, and (b) Tachai's practice.[2]

The calculation of work point based on fixed production quota comprises work contracted on annual basis or at piece rate. This form of payment of wages eliminates subjective evaluation and relates income directly to work. But, it may stress on quantity at the cost of quality and has the potential of widening the gap between the rich and the poor even without changing the ownership of the means of production. This method was introduced when preliminary and higher stage co-operatives were formed (1954-56), discontinued in 1958 but partially restored in 1962. It came under attack in the mid-1960s but was re-introduced in 1971. In some areas it was suppressed during 1974-76.

The method of distribution of income based on "from each according to his ability and to each according to his work", experimented by a hundred-odd peasants in Tachai (Dazhai), located at Taihang mountain of Shanxi, for quite some time became the guiding star. To delve into a little bit of its history, Tachai is an area of about 800 mu, divided into 4700 small, fragmented plots, scattered over mountain slope, gully and ridge, having more than twenty degrees in inclination, without irrigation and drainage facilities. The climate is harsh with temperature gliding to twenty degrees Celsius below zero in winter. Its development began in 1962. It realised high yield from small and marginal holdings at a time when the nation was recovering from the aftermath of the Great Leap Forward and the search was on for an agricultural policy, which could induce the peasants with reasonable personal incentive. Though doubts were aired about the validity of its claims, after enquiry it was upheld as a model in 1965 as: "Tachai spirit is the self-reliant spirit of working thriftily, diligently, skilfully and steadily by relying on collective strength of people's commune".[3] This method of income distribution, "to each according to work" provided ample scope to personal initiative and acted as a major incentive to raise agricultural production in backward areas and break the cyclics of poverty. It was basically a dual mode of income distribution, combining money wage and free supply of food and other essential items.

Before the establishment of the communes, a number of laws were enacted for empowerment of the women. These included land rights and the right to seek divorce. Also, there were a few women occupying senior managerial position in the commune administration. Yet, it practiced a policy of differential wage rate between sexes. Both the methods of income distribution, viz., the fixed production quota and "to each according to work", accorded lower work point to women than men for the same work, even as the first Constitution (1954) stated, "women in the People's Republic of China enjoy equal status with men in the sphere of political, economic, cultural, social and domestic life".[4] Perhaps this was not adequate. The 1982 Constitution specifically states: "the state protects the rights and interests of women and applies the principle of equal pay for equal work to men and women alike".

Distribution of Food

The supply constraint made equity in food distribution essential to tackle malnutrition and hunger. By the end of 1955, foodgrain was rationed in the urban areas; the foodgrain ration (which includes potato, corn, millet, sorghum and other coarse grains besides rice and wheat) varied between 15 and 25 kilograms per household per month, depending on their nature of work.[5] Other food items such as meat, eggs and vegetables were brought under rationing later.

The food distribution mechanism in rural areas was different. Here, comparing the output and demand requirement of foodgrain of a normal year, the households were classified into three categories as surplus, self-sufficient and deficient. The status of foodgrain surplus households was kept unchanged for a minimum period of three years. The other two categories of households faced yearly review. A household in self-sufficient category was not allowed to buy foodgrain from the State. But, it was free to sell a part of its produce to meet other needs. As an incentive to increase production, the incremental output from opening up of wasteland was not taken into account for three years in the calculation of surplus for state purchase.[6] The State assumed the responsibility to supply foodgrain to the deficient households. The quantum of state supply, however, differed regionally; in the interior and backward areas it was almost half of that of the developed areas. The transfer of foodgrain from surplus to deficit areas to meet the ration was used as a last resort since that might slacken the strive towards regional self-sufficiency.

The food rationing in rural areas took a different shape under commune. The collectives estimated the quantum of foodgrain available for distribution among its members as consumption. This quantum was distributed per unit of work point earned by its members. The quantum of food ration in the communes thus depended mainly on the size of its harvest.

III
Growth and Equity under Commune

The performance of the commune organisation to secure a higher standard of living in rural areas can be assessed from the average level of income and its equity in class distribution. Gross income in the commune originates from collective, centralised management, economic association, family business, contracted collective production and sideline occupation. Net income is obtained by deducting family business expense, taxes, depreciation of productive fixed asset and gift to friends and relatives, from the gross income. Income is divided into productive and non-productive according to its source. Income originating from agriculture, industry, transport, construction and commerce are known as productive income. Income accruing from state financial administration, collective public welfare fund or accumulation fund including wage income, subsidy, relief and remittances from friends and relatives are the sources of non-productive income. Non-productive income is mainly redistributive in nature.

The average income from the commune organisation remained stagnant between 1956, when it was introduced in the form of collective ownership of the means of production and distribution (advanced agricultural co-operative societies), and 1978, when the economic reform was initiated. Per capita yearly income of peasants increased from 73 Yuan in 1957 to 134 Yuan in 1978. Taking into account the erosion in income due to price inflation (averaging 1.1 percent per year for all commodities and 1.6 percent per year for food items in 1957-78) the per capita annual income in 1978 at 1957 prices works out to 95 Yuan. This implies a real rate of growth of 1.3 percent per year in 1957-78.[7] The realised growth rate of per capita income is modest and lower than many developing countries where planning is less centralised and regulated.

Table 3.2: Source of Rural Income

(Yuan, per capita yearly)

Source	*1957*		*1978*	
1. Collective	43.40	(59.5)	88.53	(66.3)
2. Sideline Production	21.46	(29.4)	35.79	(26.8)
3. Other Non-Borrowing	8.09	(11.1)	9.25	(6.9)
Total	72.95	(100.0)	133.57	(100.0)

Note : The figures is brackets indicate percentage to total income.
Source: *Statistical Yearbook of China* 1984, p. 471. State Statistical Bureau, Beijing.

The source of rural income given in Table 3.2 shows that between 1957 and 1978, the share of income from the collectives increased while that of sideline production and other non-borrowing income reduced. The singular emphasis on foodgrain production by the collectives linked the growth of rural income directly to agriculture. The agriculture in turn, was dominated by foodgrain production. But, the yield of foodgrain in the communes depended on a number of factors such as, (a) fertility of land, (b) location, *i.e.*, plain or hilly region and in warm or cold zone, and (c) amount of rainfall. Foodgrain production as a result, differed widely within the communes. The yield of foodgrain of several communes in Shaanxi, Gansu, Ningxia, Nei Monggol, Qinghai and Shanxi was 170 jin per mu. In many areas within the commune the yield was as low as 30 to 50 jin. Around half of the area under cultivation in Hebei, Shandong and Henan are susceptible to low yield of foodgrain. The variation in foodgrain yield in Hubei is wide, from about 250 jin per mu to 1000 jin per mu. Inter-brigade variation in foodgrain yield is estimated as ten times, ranging from 100 jin per mu to 1000 jin per mu. The daily wage in these production brigades range from one-fifth of a Yuan to three Yuan and yearly per capita income from 20 Yuan to 300 Yuan. There are plenty of such examples in the country.[8]

The foodgrain production between the poor counties was also unequal. The production in the 121 poor counties scattered over ten low yield and food deficit provinces is so uneven that 77 percent of their production comes from forty five counties and 23 percent from the other seventy six counties.[9] The yield rate of foodgrain in ninety one prefectures located in ten summer grain provinces show very low yield in forty nine prefectures.

Low land availability is not necessarily a constraint to growth in agricultural income. Average per capita land availability in Wuxian county, Liaoning is one mu. Within the county, it ranges from 1.5 mu to 2.0 mu in the east and 0.7 mu to 0.8 mu in the west. The land availability is about one-fifth of a mu in Gaixian county, Liaoning. Agricultural income in these counties increased considerably in the 1970s. In contrast, income in ten counties in Anhui with a per capita land availability of 2 mu remained much lower than the level required for subsistence mainly due to low productivity in agriculture.[10]

The regional disparity in growth and development is mirrored in the relatively faster growth of income in the areas around the industrial cities. The increase in income in these areas owed primarily to the growth of the commune and brigade enterprises. Most of these enterprises started as agricultural machine repair and manufacturing plants within the commune in order to cater agricultural mechanisation.

The growth of these enterprises depended on their proximity to industrial centres and as a result, the income generation from the communes and brigade enterprises in the sub-urban areas was much higher than those in the interiors. In the late 1970s, the average annual income from the commune and brigade enterprises was: (a) 300 Yuan in the sub-urban counties of Shanghai, (b) 100 to 180 Yuan in the sub-urban counties of Tianjin, Beijing and Jiangsu, and (c) less than 20 Yuan in ten provinces, *viz.*, Guangxi, Shaanxi,

Qinghai, Gansu, Yunnan, Xinjiang, Sichuan, Anhui, Guizhou and Xizang.[11] The situation was similar in 1981 as the per capita annual income in more than one-fifth (21.5 percent) of the counties in Shanghai and one-tenth (10 percent) of the communes around Beijing was 300 Yuan. In contrast, the per capita annual income did not exceed 300 Yuan in any of the counties of fifteen provinces and in twelve provinces the per capita income exceeded 300 Yuan in only 1 to 6 percent of the counties.

The distribution of income at each of the three tiers of the commune organisation is found to be skewed around a low mean. A near census of the 5.01 million production teams in 1976 given in Table 3.3 show that the average income of the richest 25 percent of the production teams is 3.8 times of that of the poorest 25 percent. The per capita income of the peasants in bottom 25 percent of the basic accounting units is one-tenth of the average whereas half of the total income accrues to top 25 percent of the production teams.

Table 3.3: Distribution of Production Teams in 1976

	Per Capita Income (Yuan, Yearly)	*Average Income (Yuan, Yearly)*	*Production Team (percent)*
1.	0-40	37	16.1
2.	41-50	46	11.4
3.	51-80	66	31.7
4.	81-100	91	15.6
5.	100 +	147	25.2
6.	All Classes	83	100.0

Source: 1. Shi Shan, *Nongye Jingji Wenti*, No. 2, 1980, pp. 33-36, Beijing.
2. Wu Xiang, *Renmin Ribao*, in Chinese, 5 November 1980, p. 2.

There was another census in 1980, which recorded 5.3 million production teams in the country.[12] A summary of the 1980 census reveals the following:

(a) Per capita annual income of 40 percent of the production teams (about 2.1 million production teams in the country) is less than 60 Yuan, which is close to one-third of the poverty line. Thus, the standard of living in these production teams may be quite distressing.

(b) About half a million production teams (which is about 10 percent of the production teams in the country) enjoyed the fruits of development as their per capita annual income exceeded 150 Yuan.

Per capita income of 10 percent of the communes remained less than 50 Yuan per year (which is about one-third of the poverty line) in three successive years, 1977-79. In 1976, per capita annual income of 42.8 percent of the production brigades was less than 50 Yuan. In 1978, per capita annual income of 29.6 percent of the production brigades was less than 50 Yuan and the same of 40 percent of the communes and production brigades was below 60 Yuan. The per capita income of only a few production teams exceeded 150 Yuan per year, which being the poverty line is considered to be barely just adequate for a living.[13]

The counties present a similar scenario. In 1979, the per capita yearly income is less than 50 Yuan in 16.3 percent of the counties while the same exceed 100 Yuan in 23.7 percent of the counties. Per capita yearly income of 300 Yuan was necessary to provide a good living in 1980, which only 22 of the two thousand and odd counties (0.8 percent of all the counties) in the country enjoyed.

The extent and regional spread of the non-poor counties bears a testimony of development under the commune. In 1978, all the counties in Beijing and Shanghai, the two major cities, were non-poor. About 70 percent of the counties in Heilongjiang, Tianjin and Jilin and about 40 percent of the counties in Zhejiang, Qinghai, Inner Mongolia, Ningxia and Xinjiang were non-poor. The regional concentration in this respect is apparent, as the non-poor counties are from the major cities or in the sub-urban regions and close to large and medium cities.

Before the formation of communes, equity in rural areas was sought to be achieved by distributing equally the productive assets. A major example was land, which was distributed among the landless. But the transfer of material resources of the peasants to the collectives, without compensation, had made the route to equity under commune organisation direct. The communes preferred to distribute the return from the asset equally rather than the asset itself. This eliminated inequality in the inter-personal income arising from labour productivity within the basic accounting unit and shifted the focus of equity from inter-personal to inter-accounting unit, which initially was the commune, then the production brigade and finally, the production team.

The resource endowment in the collectives vary and so also the output-labour ratio. The income in the collectives depends on the quantity of produce, which, being determined by land availability and labour productivity, gave rise to wage and income differential. The production teams with high yield in agriculture could save and invest and enjoyed a better standard of living than others. The disparity between the production teams widened as agricultural production in high income and resource rich teams increased more than the resource-poor ones. Thus, the commune could not ensure sufficient insulation from inequality. The form of labour determined the way of life. The imprimatur of redistribution of the resources from the richer production teams to assist the poorer ones could not diminish income inequality and the disparity in the level of living between the poorer and the richer teams remained pronounced. Labour as a factor input determined inter-personal inequality within the collectives and factor endowment dictated inter-collective inequality. The income differential between the collective economic units was far greater than between the workers and the peasants within a unit.

IV
The Epitome

The communes aimed to eliminate the difference between intellectual and physical labour and the disparity in the level of living between industrial worker and agricultural labourer in an agrarian economy where quality of land, *inter alia,* the yield of foodgrain shaped the level of income. Foodgrain yield rate in the communes also acted as the prime mover of income inequality and in the disparity in level of living. The differential output-labour ratio among the production teams and the ability of the resource rich collectives to retain bulk of their incremental income for ploughing them back to investment, created a general pattern of inequality in the countryside similar to those observed in low income developing countries belonging to market economy. Redistribution of factor input produced only limited results. The communes enjoyed immense power to allocate costly and scarce agricultural inputs such as high yielding variety of seed and chemical fertiliser to the areas of low yield or less resourceful communes. On many occasions, to keep an eye on the size of harvest, which the country needed so desperately to minimise food import, such redistributive policies had to be relaxed. Because of supply constraint of these inputs, foodgrain production could have suffered a setback in the event of their diversion to low yield areas. It was a risk, which many communes were reluctant to take, and in fact, did not take.

The emphasis in the communes was squarely on foodgrain production. Its primary job was to ensure food self-sufficiency in the sense that the production team or brigade on its own produces an amount, irrespective of type and quality, to meet the minimum requirement of its members. The concept of regional self-sufficiency in foodgrain explicitly stated that collective economic units should be able to produce enough to meet its own requirement before embarking on alternative activity. Since foodgrain output was the main criterion to judge the performance of commune organisations, the race to attain regional self-sufficiency in foodgrain production ignored the allied activities of agriculture such as, animal husbandry, forestry and diversified economy. Even the areas recognised for cash crop were switched to foodgrain. Its consequence was a gradual erosion of regional self-sufficiency in foodgrain as evidenced in the decline in the flow of foodgrain from surplus to deficit areas and also from the increase in the flow to food deficit areas. The number of food surplus provinces reduced from twenty in 1953 to seven in 1981. The seven food surplus provinces are: Jilin, Anhui, Hunan, Henan, Jiangsu, Zhejiang and Jiangxi. The number of food deficit provinces increased from eight to twenty during the same period and the production and requirement in two provinces *viz.*, Hubei and Guangxi, matched.

There was a general decline in the efficiency indicators. Though agricultural fixed assets in 1978 was about five and a half times more than that in 1957, labour productivity rose by about one per cent annually in 1952-78 and declined by 0.20 percent annually in 1957-78 (*i.e.*. in the commune regime). In the basic accounting units, the ratio of income to fixed assets declined from 2.37 percent in 1957 to 1.29 percent in 1978, and the ratio of net income to expenditure from 2.78 percent to 1.83 percent.[14]

The rural economy from the exclusive dependence on agriculture and more so on farming was trapped in the vicious circle of underdevelopment. The agriculture as such was unable to provide full employment to the entire rural work force, burdening it with surplus manpower. The communes preferred to keep everybody underemployed rather than some unemployed. Agricultural mechanisation was avoided due to dearth of alternative employment of surplus agricultural labour and inadequacy of investment. The income of the developed communes clearly owes more to industry, and particularly, to agro-based and rural industry and is less dependent on farming. The source of income in forty six relatively developed counties reveal that 24.9 percent of its total earnings is derived from farming, 5.8 percent from animal husbandry, 5.3 percent from fishery, 3.6 percent from other sources and an exorbitant 60.4 percent from industry.[15] However, such developed counties were few and far between.

There were islands of egregious poverty within communes mainly arising from the inability of the local economies to participate in the wider growth process due to historical reasons and thereby failing to get adequate benefit from the overall growth process. The work point system, used to distribute commune income among its members lacked allocative efficiency and its calculation remained a bone of contention forever. The commune management being confronted with the trade-off between growth and social justice landed too much on social justice without bothering about what was happening to growth. The economic growth that bids good-bye to social justice is untenable and transient. The issue is: how to guarantee the desired rate of economic growth commensurate with social justice. It could not be addressed squarely as the planners failed to realise that developmental planning is an all embracing process, which cannot be compartmentalised and that elimination of poverty and inequality is not possible merely by redistributing existing wealth.

The central intellectual mistake in the central planning is the assumption that the model for planning and development is a matter of making decisions at the top and then issuing order downwards. It was a remote, centralised, bureaucratic system imposed on a vast country of widely differing levels of economic development, which worked as a recipe for inefficiency and stagnation.

REFERENCES

1. Lung Lin. *People's Daily,* 16 October 1972.
2. Kuo-Hsiu-Sheng and Kao Hsien-Sung. *People's Daily,* 2 December 1978.
3. Red *Flag,* 1 January 1965, Beijing; *New China News Agency,* 7 August 1967; *People's Daily,* Editorial, 1 November 1965.
4. Wan Hanzhi, *Nongcun Gongzuo Tongxun,* No. 10, 5 October 1980, pp. 25-28, Beijing.
5. *New China News Agency,* 25 August 1955, Beijing.
6. *China News Service,* 26 June 1969.
7. Zhan Wu and Lin Wenpu. "Agriculture", in Yu Guangyuan (ed), *China's Socialist Modernisation,* Foreign Languages Press, Beijing, 1984, p. 262.
8. Xin Naiquan, *Renmin Ribao,* 5 March 1981, p. 3, Beijing; *Wuhan Hubei* Provincial Service in Mandarin 1100 GMT 25 July 1980; Han Leng, *Renmin Ribao,* 27 May 1980, p. 2; *Renmin Ribao,* 17 February 1981, p. 2, Beijing; *Renmin Ribao,* 27 January 1980, p. 2, Beijing; Lu Jianjhang, Gao Shangquan, Ni Di and Ma Liping, *Jingji Gunali,* 15 January 1980, pp. 29-32; Tan Keliang and Tao Yuerui, *Jingji Yanjiu,* No. 4, 20 April 1980, pp. 69-72; Zheng Yizheng, *Fujian Ribao,* 12 June 1981, p. 1, Fujian; Bai Rubing, *Red Flag,* No. 7,1 April 1982, pp. 15-19.
9. Dong Dalin and Bao Tang, *Renmin Ribao,* 26 November 1978, p. 2, Beijing.
10. Lu Shijian, *Guangming Ribao,* 11 September 1979, p. 2, Beijing; *Renmin Ribao,* 16 October 1982, p. 2, Beijing.
11. Xue Muqiao, *China's Socialist Economy,* Foreign Languages Press, Beijing, Second Edition, 1986, pp. 37 and 92; Gu Songnian and Ren Xinbao, *Nongye Jingji Wenti,* No. 7, 1982, pp. 40-44; Wang Gengjin and Zhu Rongji, *Jingji Gunali,* No. 3, 1979, pp. 21-23; Shen Jiyan, *Jingji Yanjiu,* No. 2, 20 February 1979, pp. 44-48, Beijing.
12. Xu Muqio, *op. cit,* p. 91.
13. Shi Shan, *Nongye Jingji Wenti,* No. 2. 1980, pp. 33-36, Beijing; Zhan Wu, *Jingji Gunali,* No. 9, 25 September 1979, pp. 11-17. Beijing; Xu Xin, *Guangming Ribao,* 14 February 1981, p. 4, Beijing; *Nongcun Gongzuo Tongxu,* No. 10, 5 October 1981, p. 3, Beijing; Wu Xiang, *Renmin Ribao,* in Chinese, 5 November 1980, p. 2, Beijing; Wang Changbo, *Gongsu Caiwu,* No. 8, 6 August 1981, pp. 4-12, Beijing; *Beijing Xinhua,* Domestic Service in Mandarin, 0811 GMT, 29 September 1981.
14. Zhan Wu, Nongye *Jingji Wenti,* No. 6, 1980, p. VI. II-2 to VIII-7; Zhan Wu and Lin Wenpu, *op. cit.,* p. 266.
15. *Gongshu Caiwu,* No. 7, 1982, pp. 17-23, Beijing.

4

Poverty and Inequality

Poverty alleviation is an acid test of planning in the developing countries. Precise information about the incidence of poverty, location of the poor and the economic circumstances under which they live are essential to formulate pro-poor development strategy and to make the policy towards poverty reduction effective. Even though poverty and poor people have been around the globe for aeons, its measurement remains a complex job in the absence of a universally accepted definition of poverty. The problem is compounded in a country of such diverse characteristics of the population as in case of China. Considering the pros and cons, the incidence of poverty in China has been computed from a method known for its simplicity and user-friendliness.

I
Incidence of Poverty

The Methodology

The incidence of poverty is measured by the poverty ratio (also known as head-count ratio), which is defined as the percentage of persons (or families) in the total population (families), unable to attain the income or expenditure set by the poverty line. The poverty line denotes the level of income or consumption, which is necessary to meet the minimum food requirement conforming to biological need along with specified quantity of non-food items such as clothing, shelter, transport, etc.

In the low-income developing countries with considerable

dependence on agriculture, per capita income or consumption can justifiably be used to separate poor from the total population as long as they include own production, which is important for the poor. Between income and consumption, the latter has been found to be more appropriate for analysis of poverty in the developing countries precisely for the reason that it reflects more accurately the people's actual level of well-being, while income data are more concerned with people's potential level of living. The preference for consumption is also due to the fact that the poor in most developing countries receive subsidised goods and services from the State. But, the definition of poverty based on income or consumption fails to capture the dimensions of welfare relating to socio-economic indicators such as, health, life expectancy and access to public goods.

Besides, the poverty ratio tends to reduce the incidence of poverty through adjustment at the margin, regardless of the change in the income of those within the poverty segment. Small and marginal farmers, who constitute a large chunk of the poor in the developing countries, may be worse-off in real terms, consequent upon increase in the market price of foodgrain. This may not always be reflected in the poverty ratio as much as it is insensitive to inequality in the income or consumption distribution of the poor. The poverty ratio does not change in the event of income transfer within the poor group. Nevertheless, the way poor are defined in terms of a cut-off level of income or consumption, the estimates of the incidence of poverty measured through poverty ratio provide a good indicator of its average level and enables inter-temporal and inter-regional comparison.

Poverty Ratio in 1978

The incidence of rural poverty in 1978 is estimated from the household income distribution obtained from nationwide sample survey, given in Table 4.1. Using per capita yearly income of 150 Yuan as the poverty line, 64.9 percent of rural households are estimated as poor in 1978. The percentage of persons below poverty line is more (close to 70 percent), as the average size of poor household is higher than that of non-poor. One-third of the households (57 million households) are in extreme poverty as their income is less than two-third of poverty line (100 Yuan). The size of rural poor is about half a billion (515 million) in 1978, which exceeds the addition to country's total population since 1949. About half of the poor (265 million) remained in extreme poverty.

Table 4.1: Income Distribution in Rural Areas

	Per Capita Income (Yuan, Yearly)	*Percentage of Families*
1.	0-100	33.2
2.	100-150	31.7
3.	150-200	17.6
4.	200-300	15.0
5.	300-500	1.9
6.	500 +	0.6

Source: 1. Du Runsheng, *China's Rural Economic Reform,* Foreign Languages Press, Beijing, 1989, p. 88.
2. Beijing Xinhua in English 0109 GMT 29 September 1984.

The poverty ratio is extremely sensitive to the choice of the poverty line. In view of this, the accuracy of the poverty line used above is checked from alternative sources. The poverty line in 1982 has been quantified as per capita annual income of 200 Yuan with subsidised basic needs.[1] The conversion of the poverty line of 1982 to 1978 prices require the information on price changes of the commodities specifically consumed by the poor. There are two types of prices in China, *viz.,* list price and negotiated or unplanned price. The list price is planned by the State. The negotiated price is decided between the buyer and seller. Only a few non-essential items and farm products in excess of state purchase quota come under the purview of negotiated price. These are not regulated by the state but for their unusual rise. The state control on negotiated price, if necessary, is implemented through administration of market and public supervision. The list price, being controlled by the State, is kept at a pre-determined level and remains lower than the negotiated price. The increase in list price between 1952 and 1979 is 30.9 percent in case of all commodities. These prices, though are not strictly applicable for the poor, can be used as a close approximation. Based on the list price inflation rate between 1978 and 1982, the poverty line of 150 Yuan in 1978 turns out to be 200 Yuan, which is the poverty line in 1982.

The income distribution in 1978 given above can be used to assert that in rural areas, the benefits of planned economic development percolated to only 17.5 percent of the families (30 million families) as their per capita income exceeded 200 Yuan per year. Importantly, 0.6 percent of the families (one million families) can be termed as rich as their per capita annual income exceeded 500 Yuan. The epicurean lifestyle of these one million families contrasted sharply with the terrible privation of 57 million families whose per capita income fell short of two-third of the poverty line.

Poverty in China, unlike in other developing countries, is area-specific rather than person- or family-specific. In developing countries, generally the areas are a mix of poor and non-poor, whereas in China the whole area, demarcated as the basic accounting unit in the commune administration, is either poor or non-poor. Personal or family characteristics hardly influence the poverty in China as the inter-personal income differential within a basic accounting unit can arise only due to the difference in the amount of labour put in the communes. The spread of social service such as education and heath care also was accounting team specific, thus allowing little scope of inter-personal income inequality within the accounting unit. Poverty arises as a result of inequality between the accounting units, which is mainly the outcome of differential factor endowment. In China, poor areas are more or less concomitant with poor population and poverty is known to be concentrated in areas without proper communication network, proximity to market and absence of industries, small or large. The physical conditions such as topography and rainfall are also important barometers of poverty. A large proportion of the poor live in arid areas where agricultural productivity is low and income fluctuates with the amount of rainfall.

The dependency ratio, which is defined as the number of non-workers supported by each worker is an important determinant of the level of affluence of a family. The dependency ratio in the poor families is high. The average household size in rural areas is 4.6 persons for all population; the average size of the poor and the non-poor households being 5 and 3.95 persons respectively. Each worker in the poor household has to support 2.5 persons as against 1.3 persons in the non-poor household. Thus, each worker in the poor household has to support an additional person as compared to the non-poor household. The income of the collective economic units, which is the principal source of rural income, depended on its resource availability, which differed across the regions. The resource rich units escaped the wrath of poverty. A considerable share of income of the non-poor households accrued from commune and brigade enterprises. The poor households earned very little from such enterprises. Their activities were least diversified and income from non-farm activity was meagre. They did not possess the requisite skill and access to the means of production, necessary to derive benefit from the growth process.

II
Income Inequality

The inequality in income and wealth arising from feudal rights and land tenures were abolished with the establishment of the Republic. The investment and fiscal policies, social and public services, redistribution of income from the richer to the poorer production teams and institutional changes were devised in such a way that the fruits of growth are distributed equally at personal and regional levels. And, to ensure equity in the distribution of income and wealth, regimentation was made central to the edifice. But, an egalitarian society eluded the planners and for that matter, the people mainly because of differential labour productivity, both sectorally, primarily between agriculture and industry, and regionally, between developed and backward areas. The development process came to be associated with inequality in the distribution of per capita income and consumption and in turn, in the levels of living and quality of life. However, the inter-personal inequality in the distribution of income within a small administrative unit such as production team (consisting of about 30 families) was not pronounced. The difference in the average income of the production teams caused inter-personal income inequality within the country.

The Basis

The transfer of income and asset from the rich to the poor was used as the key to equity. The massive redistribution of land, the major asset in rural areas, provided the basis. Its role in raising incomes of the rural poor and thereby reducing disparity in rural income distribution was undisputed.

Land reform is a policy viewed as zero-sum game where some benefit only because others lose. The policies that make important power groups in a society a clear loser are resisted fiercely. The land reform was violent enough to cost about half a million lives. A great loss no doubt, but it was instrumental in confiscating 700 million mu (46.6 million hectares) of land from the landlords and rich peasants and its distribution among 300 million small farmers and landless labourers.[2] Though a definite conclusion can not be arrived at on the basis of published facts and figures, it is widely felt that the land reform achieved its target with a much reduced scale of violence and disruption that accompanied the collectivization movement in agriculture in the former Soviet Union. The land reform in China enabled 60 percent of the rural population to gain access to agricultural land at the expense of 4 percent of the population. The ownership of 46.5 percent of cultivable land along with draught animal and agricultural implement exchanged hands. The reform neither eliminated private ownership of land nor pursued a perfect egalitarian distribution.

The land reform maintained a balanced approach to the issue of growth and equity and thus was able to create the necessary economic. social and institutional framework essential for agricultural development. It was successful in destroying the economic and social might of the rural elite who wielded their authority and power through possession of agricultural land. The rich peasants and landlords were dislodged from their ivory tower. But, the establishment of communes in 1958 heralded the switch over from individual or private ownership to state ownership of land and other productive assets excepting small private plots, whose size varied with land availability and density of population in the area. The regional disparity in income and consumption was not ruled out since the income in the communes depended primarily on its resource endowment. Also, since the wages in the commune were geared to man-hour of work, the possibility of inter-personal income differential within an analogous area was not ruled out.

The basis of income inequality in the urban areas differed from the rural areas. Although about 10 percent of the people lived in urban areas by 1978, its role in income and employment generation and also for providing opportunities for growth was important enough to impact on the policy of egalitarianism. However, there was never any attempt to equalize the income in urban areas in the manner it was approached in the rural areas. Most of the urban income earners were employed in industry which in terms of ownership pattern were grouped into two categories as: state ownership and collective ownership. The state-owned industries were large units and included the key industries. The largest ones were directly operated and managed by the concerned Ministry of the central government while the relatively smaller ones were under the charge of the provincial administration or under joint management of the central and provincial government. The collective owned enterprises (also known as owned by the workers) were generally small-scale units. The majority of the workers (not less than two-third at any point of time) were employed in the state-owned industries. The employees of the state-owned industries were paid wages in a structured pay scale along with benefits such as free health care, subsidized housing, transport, etc. The wages and these benefits differed both between the different categories of employees within an industry, and also between the different categories of industries. Importantly, the wages of the workers in the collective owned enterprises was considerably lower than that in the state-owned industries.

The Pattern

The State regulated the average level of income by setting the size of accumulation in the state plan. The incomes policy tolerated variation in per capita income due to quantum of work. The differential labour productivity in industry and agriculture culminated in per capita income differential between industrial workers and peasants. Inter-personal income inequality in rural areas cropped up from the divergence in resource endowment across regions. The factor endowment in the collectives was the prime mover of differential labour productivity and as a consequence output. This regional inequality, in its due turn, created inequality in the distribution of personal income. The disparity between highest and lowest wages for workers in urban areas was four times, and ten times with white collared employees included.[3]

The extent of inter-personal income inequality measured from the fractile-wise income shares obtained from the survey on income distribution show that in rural areas, the share of income of the poorest and the richest 20 percent families in 1978 is 7 percent and 41 percent respectively. Before 1978 such data in urban areas, available only for the year 1964, show that the share of income of the poorest and the richest 20 percent families as 14 percent and 33 percent respectively. The per capita income differential between poorest and richest 10 percent of the families is six times in rural areas in 1978 and about three times in urban areas in 1964. Per capita income differential between the poorest and the richest 20 percent families is two and a half times in urban areas as compared to about six times in rural areas.

The inequality in the distribution of personal income in rural and urban areas during the period of central planning in China as indicated above are not different from those in most of the low or middle income countries where the Government earmarked a role for itself in planning and development and influenced the economic activities. But, private sector played a major role and planning in these countries had a heavy dependence on market whose development took place under the watchful eyes of the Government.

III
Poverty and Inequality in the Regions

The assessment of poverty and inequality in the regions during the period of central planning is rather difficult due to non-availability of the data on income distribution before 1978. Income distribution surveys at the provincial level have been conducted since the early

1980s. As the distributional change is a rather slow process, idea about the extent of inequality in the distribution of inter-personal income and also of the incidence of poverty in the central planning regime can be had at the provincial level from the class distribution of income obtained from these surveys. A few of them are outlined below.

Jilin: Per capita income in rural areas of Jilin is 33.6 percent more than the national average in 1978. The per capita annual income of 26.4 percent families is less than 150 Yuan.[4] This makes at least one-fourth of the families in the province as poor. The standard of living in general remained at subsistence level as 87.4 percent of income is spent on food, fuel and clothing. The underlining message is that a province with per capita income greater than the national average by one-third spends almost the entire income for mere survival.

Shanxi: Per capita income in rural areas of Shanxi is about three-fourth of the national average. It increased by more than 25 percent between 1978 and 1980 and yet, the percentage of poor families in rural areas remained at 44.8 percent. In 1980, the per capita income differential between the richest and poorest quartile of the families is 4.2 times and that between the poorest and the richest half of the families is three times. The food ration in its several counties is as low as six kilogram per person per month.[5] In view of the inverse association between the per capita income and the incidence of poverty, it can be inferred that the percentage of poor families in the province in 1978 was more than that in 1980.

Liaoning: The per capita annual income of 28.4 percent of the rural families in Liaoning is less than 200 Yuan in 1980 and that of 6.3 percent of the families exceeds 500 Yuan.[6] The per capita income differential between the poorest and richest 30 percent of the families is four times.

Jiangsu: In Jiangsu, per capita annual income of 26.4 percent of the families in rural areas is less than 100 Yuan in 1978.[7] These people live below two-third of the poverty line and hence are in acute poverty.

Anhui: Intra-production brigade disparity in the average income in Anhui is evident from the per capita income of its two production teams in 1977, given in Table 4.2.

Table 4.2: Income in Chuxian Prefecture of Anhui

(Yuan per capita yearly)

Production Team	*Year*	*Production Team Average*	*Richest Household*	*Poorest Household*
1. Xiaogang	1977	35	88	6.4
2. Hezhuang	1978	116	192	36
	1980	545	1146	336

Source: The Chinese Rural Development Problem Study Team. *Zhongguo Shehul Kexue,* No. 3, 1982, pp. 73-110, Beijing.

In Chuxian prefecture, the per capita annual income of the poorest household in Xiaogang production team is about one-fifth of the average income of the production team. The per capita income in the richest household is two and a half times of the average of the production team. The income of the richest household is about fourteen times of that of the poorest.

The income inequality in Xiaogang production team in 1978 is such that: (a) per capita income of the richest household of the production team is 5.3 times of that of the poorest household, (b) per capita income of the richest production team is 65.5 percent more than the average, and (c) per capita income of the poorest household is 31 percent of the average. A much reduced level of intra-team inequality is the outcome of high growth in income.

Beijing and Gansu: A sample survey on household income and consumption was carried out in Beijing in 1981.[8] It was conducted in 1196 families consisting of 5125 persons. The average family size is 4.29, of which 2.33 are employed and 1.96 are unemployed. If 2.33 employed persons support 1.96 persons, then each employed person supports 1.96/2.33 = 0.84 person, and 1.84 persons, including him.

The family expenses in China are met by pooling the income of all the earning members. The earning members of the family are statutorily and customarily obliged to look after their superannuated members. The State extends its support for the retired persons only when family income is inadequate to meet the expenses. This makes earner-dependent ratio a prime determinant of the level of living of not only for the family, but also for the earner. A high income family normally will have a bachelor or a spinster as earner.

The average monthly income of the employed persons is 90.11 Yuan in the households belonging to the lowest average per capita expenditure (less than 15 Yuan). On the contrary, the average monthly income of employed persons is about 70 Yuan in the households belonging to the highest average per capita monthly expenditure (35 to 50 Yuan). The consumption differential between the two groups of households *viz.*, high and low per capita income, is not explained by the income differential because of the household size and more, the number of persons supported by each employed person in the household. The average size of high-income-low-consumption households is 6.71 persons as against 3.17 persons in low-income-high-consumption households. Consequently, each employed person in high-income-low-consumption household has to support 3.92 persons including himself as against 1.18 in low-income-high-consumption household.

Table 4.3: Income Distribution in Rural Areas of Beijing and Gansu

No.	*Per Capita Income (Yuan, Yearly)*	*Percentage of Families*
	Beijing : 1981	
1	0 – 150	4.2
2	150 – 300	33.9
3	300 – 400	28.6
4	400 – 500	24.0
5	500 – 1000	8.4
6	1000 +	0.9
	All Classes	100.0
	Gansu : 1982	
1	0 – 100	21.1
2	100 – 200	45.2
3	200 – 300	22.5
4	300 – 400	8.2
5	400 – 500	2.3
6	500 +	0.7
	All Classes	100.0

Source: 1. *Beijing Xinhua*, in English, 1232 GMT, 16 August, 1982.
2. Sample Survey by the Provincial Administration, Gansu.

The incidence of poverty and inequality is strikingly different in the areas benefited by industrial cities and hard-core rural areas.

It is evident from the pattern of income distribution in rural areas of Beijing, the capital city, and Gansu, an underdeveloped province in the north-western part of the country. The disparity between the two provinces is amplified in their per capita income (in rural areas), which in 1978 is 225 Yuan in Beijing as against 98 Yuan in Gansu. The per capita income of Beijing is about 70 percent more than the national average while that of Gansu is about 70 percent of the national average. This makes the former 2.3 times of the latter. Such wide disparity in the level of average income is accompanied by an equally wide disparity in its distribution at personal level. A comparison of the income distributions obtained from the sample survey conducted in rural areas of Beijing in 1981 and Gansu in 1982 given in Table 4.3 show:

(a) the per capita annual income of 61.9 percent of the families in Beijing as against only 11.2 percent of the families in Gansu exceeds 300 Yuan;
(b) the per capita annual income of 33.3 percent of the families in Beijing as against only 3 percent of the families in Gansu exceeds 400 Yuan;
(c) the per capita annual income of 9.3 percent of the families in Beijing as against only 0.7 percent in Gansu exceeds 500 Yuan;
(d) per capita annual income of more than half (52.6 percent) of the families in Beijing as against one-tenth of the families in Gansu range from 300 to 500 Yuan.

These give two clear messages about the disparity in the levels of living between the two areas. First, high income growth reduces inequality, as is the case of Beijing. Secondly, the pattern of income growth in the two provinces underlines the centre-periphery syndrome.

IV
Calorie Deficient Population

The estimate of energy intake, and more, the requirement in any developing country is fiercely debated. The intake is estimated from either food balance sheet or nationwide sample surveys. The estimate of requirement is based on population and activity profile, climate and topography of the country, etc. Besides, the very concept of minimum energy requirement has, of late, been the subject matter of an intense debate, making the task complex. In view of this, first the available estimate of intake and requirement in the country are summarised and then an estimate of calorie requirement is made from age-sex-activity distribution of the population. Comparing the requirement with the intake, the percentage of calorie deficient population is estimated for the year 1978.

Intake and Requirement of Nutrients

The estimate of the intake and requirement of nutrients made by different organisations, given in Table 4.4 differ. The decline in calorie and protein intake between 1952 and 1959 are in tune with the dip in agricultural production and overall deterioration in the standard of living following the Great Leap Forward. The calorie intake increased afterwards and the estimate of intake made by the Nutrition Survey in 1982 is more than both the 1959 estimate of the Public Health Department and the 1978 estimate of the State Statistical Bureau.

The intake of nutrient was not balanced as the proportion of cereal and vegetables in food intake remained unusually high throughout the period 1952-78. According to the State Statistical Bureau estimate, 94 percent of both calorie and protein intake originated from grain and vegetable and only 6 percent from animal products. The state of underdevelopment in agriculture, particularly of the food-producing sector is mainly responsible for this inadequacy of animal protein. For example, the estimates for China in this regard indicate that each percentage point increase in the share of animal protein requires about ten billion jin (5 million ton) of fodder grain.

Table 4.4: Intake and Requirement of Nutrients

(per capita daily)

Source of Estimate	*Year*	*Calorie (Kcal)*	*Protein (gram)*	*Fat (gram)*
A. Intake				
(a) State Statistical Bureau	1952	2270	69.6	28.3
(b) State Statistical Bureau	1978	2311	70.8	29.9
(c) Public Health Department	1959	2060	57.0	—
(d) Second Nutrition Survey	1982	2484	—	—
B. Requirement				
(a) Association of Physiology	1982	2400	75	65
(b) Planning Bureau, M/O Agriculture	1982	2465	64.4	29.9
(c) State Statistical Bureau	1982	2666	72.9	41.2

Source: 1. Wang Hengwei, *Gongyuan 2000 Nian De Zhongguo,* September 1984, Beijing.
2. Grain and Cash Crop Task Force, Chinese Academy of Agricultural Sciences.
3. *Statistical Yearbook of China,* State Statistical Bureau, Beijing, 1984, pp. 477-78, 480.

Average nutritional availability may be treated as a poor indicator of the nutritional status of the population as a whole or within groups of population, mainly due to unequal access to food supply which results in both inter- and intra-regional variation in food intake. Quality and quantity of food supply as well as intake varied considerably according to place of residence, such as urban or rural and within a region according to natural endowment. The households in the richer sub-urban and in fertile regions of south and east enjoyed better access to non-staple food. The urbanites in general enjoyed greater access to a variety of food. The location of the household determined not only the quantity but also the quality of food consumption and, in turn, the nutritional status of the population.

As in the case of intake, the average calorie requirements made by the three premier organisations in the country mentioned above differ. However, these estimates of requirement lie in a relatively narrower range than those of intake.

Calorie Requirement: An Estimate

In view of the sensitivity of the average calorie requirement of the population to the estimation of calorie deficiency, the requirement is estimated afresh here from the age-sex-activity distribution of the population coupled with their calorie norm recommended by the Food and Agriculture Organisation (FAO) of the United Nations. The population distribution is worked out from the 1982 census. Hence, the estimate of calorie requirement derived from this distribution would relate to the year 1982. However, stability of the population profile in the short term (1978-82) allows the calorie requirements for 1982 to remain valid for 1978.

The distribution of population by age, sex and activity, known as population weighting diagram, is worked out in the following way.

The entire population is grouped into less than and above fifteen years old, each for male and female. Table 4.5 gives the population proportions of below and above 15 years of age. Persons aged less than 15 years comprise children and adolescents. They are disaggregated into four age cohort, *viz.*, (a) less than four years, (b) between five and nine years, and (c) between ten and fourteen years, each for boys and girls.

Table 4.5: Population Proportions of Below and Above 15 Years of Age

No.	*Category*	*Male*	*Female*	*Total*
1	0 - 14	17.24	16.20	33.44
2	15 +	34.28	32.28	66.56
	a) Workers	29.13	22.60	51.73
	b) Non-Workers	5.15	9.68	14.83
3	Total	51.52	48.48	100.00

Source: Tables 5 and 12, p. 80-84, *Statistical Year Book of China*, State Statistical Bureau, Beijing, 1986.

Persons aged fifteen years and above are grouped into (a) workers, and (b) non-workers, separately for male and female.

The workers are classified by their activity as heavy, moderate and sedentary. Heavy workers are those engaged in farming, animal husbandry, forestry, mining, power, gas, electricity, water supply and construction. Moderate workers are those engaged in manufacturing, geological surveying, census, public health and welfare and sedentary workers are those engaged in transport, telecommunication, commerce, trade, public utility services, education and research. The activity distribution of the workers is given in Table 4.6.

Table 4.6: Activity Distribution of Workers

(Percentage)

No.	*Category*	*Male*	*Female*	*Total*
1	Heavy	84.96	90.87	87.55
2	Moderate	9.58	6.10	8.06
3	Sedentary	5.46	3.03	4.39
4	Total	100.00	100.00	100.00

Source: Employed Population by Industry, Third National Population Census, Table 12, p. 84, *Statistical Year Book of China*, State Statistical Bureau, Beijing, 1986.

The three categories of workers, the children and adolescents and the non-workers together make the population weighting diagram. This coupled with the nutritional norms set by FAO yields the average minimum calorie requirement, which is given in Table 4.7. The estimated average minimum requirement works out to 2697 calories per person per day. It is close to the norm of 2666 calorie per capita per day, estimated by the State Statistical Bureau.

The complexity of estimation of calorie norms in a country as vast and varied as China would make it appropriate to record its foreseeable limitations. The estimated calorie requirement does not take into account the supplementary needs of pre-natal and anti-natal mothers which, if considered, will make this estimate of requirement (2697 calories per capita per day) an underestimate. It would also be an underestimate if climate and topography are taken into account for a majority of the population lives in pretty cold climate for a considerable period of time in the year. The average annual temperature of thirty years (1951-80) in two-thirds of the provinces is less than fifteen degree Celsius. In ten provinces it is less than ten degree Celsius; and in sub-zero range for three months in a year in seven provinces. It has mountainous and hilly areas, where people require more calorie than those living in the plains. On the contrary, the requirement would be overstated if the workers in their respective activities do not work with full intensity. High underemployment in agriculture has the impact of overstating the true calorie need. These are certain features, some of which tend to push the average calorie needs estimated above, upwards, and some downwards.

Table 4.7: Average Calorie Requirement

Age-Sex-Activity Group	*Persons (million)*	*Persons (percent)*	*Calorie Norm*
1. *0 to 4 years*			
a. Boys	49.00	4.86	1200
b. Girls	45.67	4.53	1500
2. *5 to 9 years*			
a. Boys	56.96	5.65	2100
b. Girls	53.73	5.33	1800
3. *10 to 14 years*			
a. Boys	67.85	6.73	2500
b. Girls	63.92	6.34	2200
4. *15 years and above*			
I. Workers: Male			
a. Heavy	249.48	24.75	3900
b. Moderate	28.13	2.79	2800
c. Sedentary	16.02	1.59	2400
II. Workers: Female			
a. Heavy	207.07	20.54	3000
b. Moderate	13.91	1.38	2200
c. Sedentary	6.89	0.68	1900
III. Non-Workers			
a. Male	51.96	5.15	2400
b. Female	97.56	9.68	1900
All Population	1008.15	100.00	2697

Calorie Deficiency: An Estimate

The average calorie requirement estimated from the age-sex-activity distribution of the population is compared with the calorie intake in order to estimate the percentage of calorie deficient population. The actual intake in 1978 is taken as a simple average of the estimate of State Statistical Bureau and that obtained from the food balance sheet and associated consumption norms. This works out to about 2000 calories per person per day. Then, on the requirement side, in order to rule out possible overestimation, particularly due to underemployment in the communes, the average per capita daily requirement is scaled down to 2600 calories. Setting the average intake of 2000 calories against the requirement of 2600 calories, the average shortfall works out to 23 percent from the requirement. Clearly, prevalence of poverty and undernutrition, which is associated with deficiency in calorie intake, is not disputed. A pertinent question is: how the deficit is dispersed among the population.

Poverty, which is concerned with the absolute standard of living of a section of the society, the poor and inequality, which refers to the relative standard of living across the entire society, though different concepts, are inter-related. At maximum inequality, one person has everything and hence poverty is clearly high. At the other extreme, minimum inequality, where all are equal, is compatible with zero poverty, where no one is poor as well as with maximum poverty, where all are poor.

The pattern of distribution of the average calorie intake in China is not known. If there is perfect equity in the calorie distribution then the entire population is liable to be calorie deficient (since the average requirement is less than the average intake) and the extent of deficiency will be 23 percent for each. Under the circumstances, a few can meet their calorie need if and only if, others consume less than the average availability (which itself is 23 percent less than the requirement). Thus, for someone to attain the minimum requirement, inequality in the distribution of calorie intake must prevail. Such an eventuality reduces the proportion of calorie deficient population and at the same stroke, drives the rest to greater calorie deficiency, because, with unchanged average intake, some can overcome their deficiency only by absorbing the share of others.

The percentage of calorie deficient population in 1978 is estimated on the assumption that the distribution of per capita calorie intake follows a two parameter log-normal distribution. The log-normal distribution is specified by mean and standard deviation of per capita calorie intake of the population.[9] The parametric values of the log-normal distribution function used here are: (a) mean of the log-normal distribution is per capita daily intake of 2000 calories, (b) standard deviation of the log-normal distribution is measured from the inequality in the distribution of per capita calorie intake (assumed as Lorenz ratio of 0.10). The percentage of calorie deficient population is estimated from the above specified log-normal distribution setting the minimum requirement of 2600 calories per capita per day as cut-off point.[10] This exercise traces the percentage of calorie deficient population in 1978 to around 60 percent, which is close to the estimate of incidence of poverty.

The above estimate of the percentage of calorie deficient population depends on the assumptions and parametric values mentioned above. Among these, the assumption of log-normality in the distribution of per capita calorie intake and Lorenz Ratio of calorie distribution as 0.10 are critical, as it is not specifically tested in case of China although it has been found to be valid in many developing countries with similar per capita income and consumption. In the 1960s and 1970s, the Lorenz Ratio of per capita total consumption in rural areas of India revolved around 0.32 and that of per capita food consumption around 0.16. In this context, the Lorenz Ratio of per capita calorie intake as 0.10 used here is rather on the low side and rules out the possibility of overstating the inequality in the distribution of calorie intake and hence in the percentage of calorie deficient population.

The calorie deficiency estimated above is expressed in terms of quantity. But no less important is the qualitative aspect of this deficiency, which arises from the inability of the diets to provide all the nutrients in right amount, a phenomenon generally observed in the low-income developing countries, to which China can be no exception. The study on rural Bangladesh by Osmani is an excellent example.[11]

The poverty ratio (*i.e.*, the percentage of persons or families living below an exogenously defined poverty cut-off point) is a measure of the incidence of poverty. The percentage of the calorie deficient population, which is the ratio of persons unable to attain the minimum level of calorie requirement (in order to lead a healthy and active life) to the total population, is a measure of the nutritional status of the population. The estimate of poverty ratio is different from the calorie deficiency as the latter is definitionally more related to under-nutrition than poverty.

The relation between the rate of economic growth and the inequality in income distribution is treated as reciprocal in poverty reduction. For equity to produce meaningful result a reasonable level of income and consumption is necessary. Talk of equity in a stagnant economy makes no sense. The impact of equity on reduction of poverty and improvement in standard of living depends on a minimum rate of income and consumption growth, which could not be achieved under central planning.

REFERENCES

1. Zheng Zhongji, *Jingji Gunali,* No. 10, 15 October 1982, pp. 15-18, Beijing.
2. Ten Great Years, Beijing 1960, p. 34.
3. Xu Dixin, *op. cit,* p. 105.
4. *Changchum Jilin,* Provincial Service in Mandarin, 2200 GMT, 4 May 1981.
5. *Taiyuan Shanxi,* Provincial Service in Mandarin, 2300 GMT, 26 March 1982 and *Taiyuan Shanxi Nongmin,* 1 March, 1986, p. 1; *Nongmin Ribao,* 12 March 1986, Beijing.
6. *Shenyang Liaoning,* Provincial Service in Mandarin, 1030 GMT, 29 September 1985.
7. *Nanjing Xinhua Ribao,* in Chinese, 23 September 1982, p. 2.
8. Xiang Qiyuan, "Income Distribution", in Xu Dixin, *op. cit.,* p. 115.
9. Aitchinson, J. and Brown, J. A. C., *The Lognormal Distribution with reference to its Uses in Economics,* Cambridge University Press, 1976.
10. Datta, K. L. "A Research Note on the Analysis of Global Poverty". *Manchester Papers on Development,* Vol. III, No. 1, March 1987, pp. 71-102, Manchester, England.
11. Osmani, Siddiq R. (ed), *Nutrition and Poverty,* Oxford, Clarendon Press, 1992, and "Food Problem in Bangladesh", in Jean Dreze, Amartya Sen and Athar Hussain (eds), *op. cit.*

5

Regional Differential

China, with an area of 9.6 million square kilometres, stretching 5000 kilometres from east to west and 5500 kilometres from north to south is indeed a vast country. Only Russia and Canada surpass it in area. Area and population of its provinces are greater than most of the countries in the world. In such a big country, the national averages are more likely to mask the regional disparity. The inter-provincial disparity in the variables that comprehensively define the leading indicators of growth and development is indeed great in China; so also the spatial distribution of public services such as education, health, medicare, transport and communication.

I
Balanced Regional Development

The historical inequalities divided the country between the developed coastal areas and the backward western interior. Since all the regions are not equally endowed to take advantage of the growth opportunities planned intervention is necessary to ensure that the fruits of growth are equitably distributed across the regions. The regions and their characteristics as evident in the early years of the Republic are outlined below.

The Regions

The provinces in China are the focal point of administration. The autonomous regions and the municipalities directly under the central government are treated at par. In 1978, there were 21 provinces, five autonomous regions and three municipalities directly under the central government. The provinces and autonomous regions are divided into autonomous prefectures, counties, autonomous counties and cities. The counties and autonomous counties are divided into townships, nationality townships and towns. The municipalities directly under the central government and other large cities are divided into districts and counties. The autonomous prefectures are divided into counties, autonomous counties, and cities. However, considering the climate, topography and agricultural practices, the provinces, autonomous regions and the municipalities directly under the central government are grouped into several regions. This makes the analysis of the development pattern, region-wise, important in case of China.

Beijing, Tianjin, Hebei, Shanxi and west of Inner Mongolia comprise the north. It has mineral resources especially coal, and is industrially developed, with a sound base of iron and steel, heavy machinery, machine building, metallurgy and chemical industry. Its population is predominantly non-agricultural.

The north-east comprises Liaoning, Heilongjiang, Jilin and east of Inner Mongolia. It has oil reserves and iron ore deposits. Its agriculture is mechanised and industrial base consists of iron and steel, machinery, oil and chemical. It suffers from scarcity of coal, which is transported from the north. Its communication network and light industry are weak.

Shaanxi, Gansu, Qinghai, Ningxia and Xianjiang comprise the north-west. The region is multi-racial and underdeveloped. Deserts and mountains prevail over vast expanses and its agricultural farms are mostly confined to small irrigated patches of oases distributed at the foot of mountainous range. Sichuan, Guizhou, Yunnan and Tibet form the south-west. The agricultural development within the region differ enormously and so also the overall development.

Shanghai, Jiangsu, Zhejiang, Anhui, Jiangxi, Fujian and Shandong constitute the east. It contains 30 percent of the total population in 8.2 percent of area. It has the highest number of cities and a developed communication network. Its agricultural productivity is one of the highest and industrial base consists of machine building, electrical equipment, chemical and textiles. It faces scarcity of critical raw materials such as oil and coal, most of which are transported from the north.

Plateaus and mountains account for two-third of total area and plains and basins for the remaining one-third. China's diverse topography encompasses the highest and one of the lowest places on the Earth and its relief varies from nearly impenetrable mountainous terrain to vast coastal lowlands. Its climate ranges from extremely desert like conditions in the north-west to tropical monsoon in the south-west and it has the greatest contrast in temperature between the northern and southern borders of any nation in the world. Tropical and sub-tropical regions account for one-fourth of the total area.

Because of complex natural conditions, the population of China is quite unevenly distributed. Its population density varies strikingly, with greatest contrast occurring between the east and the west. Most of the high density areas are coterminous with the alluvial plains on which intensive agriculture is centered. In contrast, the isolated, extensive western and frontier regions are sparsely populated.

Towards a Regional Planning

The planning of regional economic development in the 1950s, considering the socio-economic disparity between the developed eastern coastal area and backward western interior, was framed into "coast" and "hinterland" and the provinces were classified into three broad groups based on their per capita gross output in industry and agriculture (GVOIA) as: (a) developed, constituting the provinces with per capita GVOIA more than one thousand Yuan per year, (b) average developed, with per capita GVOIA between six hundred Yuan and one thousand Yuan per year, and (c) underdeveloped, with per capita GVOIA less than six hundred Yuan per year. According to these norms, seven provinces were categorised as developed, six as average developed and sixteen as underdeveloped. Hunan, Fujian, Shaanxi, Jiangxi, Henan, Anhui and Sichuan were among the underdeveloped.

The development of hinterland was emphasised in the First Plan with the allocation of about half of total investment. In the First Plan, steel plant was set up in the interior (Nei Monggal). Also, industries were set up in central (Hubei) and south-west (Sichuan) region of the country. The share of hinterland in gross value of industrial output rose from 28 percent in 1950 to 36 percent in 1980.

Increased agricultural output, wherever it occurred, failed to raise rural income to the desired extent because of low price of farm products. This accentuated the price differential between agricultural and industrial products. The industries remained concentrated in the west and north-east. About 70 percent of the modern industries were concentrated along the east coast while 9 percent of GVOIA originated in the west.[1] Most of the railways and road construction were along the east coast and north-east. The communication network in south-west and north-west remained poor. The industrialised regions such as, Shanghai and Liaoning remitted to the central government well above half of their revenue, which was essential to subsidise the underdeveloped areas. Investment decisions being guided by efficient utilisation of capital bypassed the backward regions and continued to flow in developed areas, symbolising the development scenario of a typical low-income capital scarce economy. The diversion of managerial and technical manpower from the developed to the backward regions generally proved ineffective due to inadequate investment and infrastructure. There were initial flurry of publicity with the programmes to contain regional disparity. But, these like many others, sank into oblivion.

II
Regional Variation

Income and Food Consumption

There is perceptible inter- and intra-provincial disparity in average income and also of foodgrain consumption. In 1978, per capita yearly foodgrain consumption at provincial level ranged from 571 jin (285.5 kilogram) in Guangdong to 352 jin (176 kilogram) in Tianjin, and that of income from 290 Yuan in Shanghai to 91 Yuan in Hebei. The inter-provincial disparity measured by coefficient of variation is less in case of per capita foodgrain consumption (14 percent) than in per capita income (36 percent).

The inter-provincial disparity is such that at provincial level, the ratio between the maximum and minimum in 1981 is: (a) more than 4.0 in per capita income of basic accounting units (in rural areas), and (b) 1.6 in wages of staff and workers (in urban areas) fixed by the State under regulatory mechanism and wages in collective owned units. At the provincial level, the wages of workers and staff in urban areas was more or less uniform. It was not so in case of the per capita income of the basic accounting units in rural areas. The inter-provincial disparity measured by coefficient of variation is 38 percent in per capita income of basic accounting units and 10 percent in wages of staff and workers.

The regional differential in per capita income and expenditure is reflected in the consumption of basic items that enter into an average food basket. The real rate of income growth of the region determined not only the quantity but also the quality of the food consumption. Transport bottleneck came in the way of smooth exchange of commodities between surplus and deficit areas, and partly as a result, the regional disparity in per capita consumption of items such as edible oil, meat, sugar and poultry was considerable.

The structure of income growth and redistributive policies did not produce any salutary effect on reduction of regional disparity in per capita income and consumption. The only success lies in a relatively lesser disparity in food consumption, which is the outcome of rigorous food management. It may, of course, be argued whether the control and regulation on food production and distribution by itself is responsible for a stagnant agricultural sector.

Output and Population

An expression of regional disparity can be obtained from the divergence between the population and output shares in the provinces. The provincial shares of agriculture, industry and foodgrain output and population as given in Table 5.1 are used to assess the regional disparity in output generation.

The regional disparity in the generation of industrial output is amplified in the following:

Table 5.1: Output and Population Shares in 1981

(*Percentage*)

	Province	*POPL*	*GAOV*	*HIND*	*LIND*	*GIOV*	*GRAIN*
1.	Beijing	0.92	0.8	4.6	3.8	4.2	0.6
2.	Tianjin	0.78	0.8	3.3	4.4	3.8	0.3
3.	Hebei	5.28	4.9	4.5	3.9	4.2	4.8
4.	Shanxi	2.52	2.3	3.2	1.4	2.3	2.2
5.	Inner Mongolia	1.92	1.8	1.3	1.0	1.2	1.6
6.	Liaoning	3.56	3.6	11.5	6.1	8.7	3.6
7.	Jilin	2.25	2.5	3.1	2.1	2.6	2.8
8.	Heilongjiang	3.25	3.9	6.6	3.1	4.8	3.8
9.	Shanghai	1.18	1.4	10.3	13.1	11.8	0.6
10.	Jiangsu	6.03	9.0	7.2	10.7	9.0	7.7
11.	Zhejiang	3.87	5.1	2.9	5.2	4.1	4.4
12.	Anhui	4.95	5.0	2.3	2.7	2.5	5.5
13.	Fujian	2.58	2.5	1.2	1.9	1.6	2.5
14.	Jiangxi	3.31	3.3	1.8	1.8	1.8	3.9
15.	Shandong	7.41	8.6	6.0	7.3	6.6	7.1
16.	Henan	7.41	7.1	3.7	4.2	3.9	7.1
17.	Hubei	4.76	4.9	4.7	4.8	4.8	5.2
18.	Hunan	5.38	5.7	3.7	3.1	3.4	6.7
19.	Guangdong	5.91	5.2	3.5	6.1	4.8	5.1
20.	Guangxi	3.63	3.1	1.2	1.9	1.6	3.5
21.	Sichuan	9.93	8.3	5.3	5.3	5.3	10.7
22.	Guizhou	2.84	1.8	1.0	0.7	0.8	1.7
23.	Yunnan	3.24	2.6	1.4	1.3	1.4	2.8
24.	Shaanxi	2.88	2.2	1.9	2.1	2.0	2.3
25.	Gansu	1.95	1.2	2.3	0.6	1.4	1.3
26.	Qinghai	0.39	0.3	0.3	0.2	0.2	0.2
27.	Ningxia	0.39	0.3	0.3	0.1	0.2	0.4
28.	Xinjiang	1.30	1.5	0.9	0.7	0.8	1.2

Legend: POPL = Population, GAOV and GIOV are Gross agricultural and industrial output value. HIND and LIND are value of output in heavy and light industry. GRAIN is Foodgrain production.

Note: 1. The variables are expressed as provincial shares.
2. Population relates to 1st July 1982.
3. Full data for Xizang (Tibet) are not available. Its share of population is 0.19 percent.

Source: Estimated from *Statistical Year Book of China, 1981,* p. 19 and *Statistical Year Book of China,* 1984, p. 90, State Statistical Bureau, Beijing.

(a) Three provinces, *viz.*, Shanghai, Liaoning and Jiangsu together account for 10.8 percent of population and generate 29.5 percent of industrial output.

(b) Adding Beijing and Tianjin to it, these five provinces account for 12.5 percent of population and 37.5 percent of industrial output.

(c) With 1.18 percent of population, Shanghai accounts for 11.8 percent of industrial output.

(d) Shanghai and Liaoning with 4.7 percent of the population generate 21.8 percent of the output of heavy industry.

(e) Shanghai and Jiangsu with 7.2 percent of the population generate 23.8 percent of the output of light industry.

The industrially developed provinces also have a developed agricultural base. The five provinces mentioned in (a) and (b) above together account for 15.6 percent of agricultural production and 12.8 percent of foodgrain output. The lower share of foodgrain output as compared to agricultural output in these industrially developed provinces is explained by the non-farm activities in agriculture. These underline the fact that agricultural development is accompanied by industrial development in the regions where the agriculture is diversified and less dependent on farming. Non-farm activity indeed contributed to agricultural development through diversification of agricultural output and income, which gave a boost to industrial development. The regions enjoying the fruits of industrial development are better able to develop their agriculture. Equally true is that the growth of light industry did not bypass the regions with a diversified agriculture.

The regional disparity in output generation can be quantified by the rank correlation coefficient between their provincial shares. The value of rank correlation coefficient ranges from zero to unity. It becomes zero when the ranks of two shares are exactly opposite, and unity when the ranks are identical. A low value of rank correlation coefficient symbolises high inter-provincial disparity and *vice-versa*.

The rank correlation coefficient between the share of population and both agricultural and foodgrain output is 0.98. It reflects each region's identical emphasis on agriculture and foodgrain production, besides demonstrating the dependency of agriculture on foodgrain production.

The rank correlation coefficient between the share of population and industrial output is 0.60, and between the share of population and output of heavy and light industry are 0.54 and 0.63 respectively. These merely bring out the co-existence of provinces with low industrialisation and concentration of industries.

The high rank correlation coefficient between share of output in heavy and light industry (0.88) is indicative of their co-existence and complementarities, underlining the growth of light industry in regions with heavy industry base. The dispersal of heavy industry sometimes may be circumscribed by strategic factors. But the regional spread of light industry need not necessarily depend on heavy industry. The growth of heavy industry in a few provinces of India for example, is equally conditioned by strategic factors. India's border province of Punjab, being at a striking distance from Pakistan truly does not have a heavy industrial base and yet holds one of fastest growing light industry. This is missing in China.

The divide between the industrialized and the non-industrialized areas come to the fore from the data on population and output shares given in Table 5.1 above. Of the 28 provinces, thirteen can be classified as industrially developed. These are: Jiangsu, Zhejiang, Guangdong, Shandong, Liaoning, Beijing, Tianjin, Shanghai, Hebei, Shanxi, Jilin, Heilongjiang and Hubei. The remaining fifteen provinces are at various stages of industrialization and are industrially backward in relation to the thirteen industrially developed provinces. These fifteen may be called non-industrialized. These are: Nei Monggol, Ningxia, Xianjiang, Gansu, Qinghai, Yunnan, Guizhou, Guangxi, Anhui, Fujian, Jiangxi, Henan, Hunan, Sichuan and Shaanxi. The population and output shares of these two groups of provinces are given in Table 5.2.

The output shares in the industrialized provinces are less dispersed than in the non-industrialized provinces. The output shares of these two groups of provinces can not be directly compared in view of the difference in the number of provinces in the two groups and more, due to the difference in the population shares. For this reason, the disparity in the output shares between these two groups of provinces have been calculated after eliminating the differential shares of population in a *pro-rata* manner. After eliminating the difference, the industrial output of the two groups of provinces is observed to differ by 2.8 times. The disparity is less in case of agricultural output and virtually non-existent in the share of foodgrain output. The similar shares of foodgrain output in the industrialized and the non-industrialized provinces speak for the implementation of the policy of grain as a key link.

Table 5.2: Output Shares in Industrialized and Non-Industrialized Provinces

(Percentage)

	Industrialized Provinces	*Non-Industrialized Provinces*	*Disparity*
1. Population	47.72 (58)	52.10 (74)	-
2. GAOV	53.00 (64)	46.70 (77)	1.24
3. Heavy Industry	71.40 (50)	28.60 (73)	2.73
4. Light Industry	72.00 (59)	27.60 (81)	2.85
5. GIOV	71.70 (50)	28.10 (75)	2.79
6. Foodgrain	48.20 (64)	51.40 (85)	1.02

Notes: 1. GAOV and GIOV are gross agricultural and industrial output value respectively.
2. The figures in the brackets are coefficient of variation of the shares.

The correlation coefficient between the population and output shares in the industrialized and the non-industrialized provinces are presented in Table 5.3. The near similar and high (greater than 0.94) correlation coefficient between population share and agricultural and foodgrain output in both the industrialized and non-industrialized areas underline the seriousness with which the policy of "grain as a key link" was implemented. The correlation coefficient between the share of population and industrial output is high in the non-industrialized provinces, but extremely low in the industrialized provinces. It characterized the industrial development in provinces with relatively less population.

In the early stages of development, resource constraint comes in the way of the claims of the less developed regions. The attack on regional inequality at this stage does not seem to have great significance for planning, as the task of elevating the economy onto a higher growth path appears imperative. As a result, regions where growth potential can be developed quickly, grow more rapidly than others. With development, as additional resources are available for investment, the claims of underdeveloped regions are heeded. At this stage, transmission of growth impulses from developed to underdeveloped regions and generation of growth impulses within the underdeveloped regions can ensure reduction of regional disparity in growth and development The pattern of industrial development attests the failure to meet the claims of the less developed regions.

Table 5.3: Correlation Matrix of Population and Output Shares in Industrialized and Non-Industrialized Provinces

	POPL	*GAOV*	*HIND*	*LIND*	*GIOV*	*GRAIN*
I. Industrialized Provinces						
POPL	1.00	0.94	0.00	0.20	0.12	0.96
GAOV		1.00	0.07	0.33	0.23	0.98
HIND			1.00	0.64	0.88	0.03
LIND				1.00	0.93	0.20
GIOV					1.00	0.13
GRAIN						1.00
II. Non-Industrialized Provinces	POPL	GAOV	HIND	LIND	GIOV	GRAIN
POPL	1.00	0.98	0.93	0.97	0.97	0.98
GAOV		1.00	0.92	0.98	0.97	0.99
HIND			1.00	0.92	0.97	0.93
LIND				1.00	0.98	0.97
GIOV					1.00	0.98
GRAIN						1.00
III. All Provinces	POPL	GAOV	HIND	LIND	GIOV	GRAIN
POPL	1.00	0.94	0.30	0.38	0.35	0.97
GAOV		1.00	0.39	0.51	0.48	0.96
HIND			1.00	0.82	0.95	0.31
LIND				1.00	0.96	0.39
GIOV					1.00	0.37
GRAIN						1.00

Note: Legends are in Table 5.1.

West *vs.* Rest

The western region of China consisting of Guangxi, Sichuan, Guizhou, Yunnan, Xizang on the south and Shaanxi, Gansu,

Qinghai, Ningxia, Xinjiang and west of Nei Monggol on the north, is relatively underdeveloped as compared to the east which comprise seven coastal provinces besides Beijing, Tianjin and Shanghai and the central region consisting of Heilongjiang, Jilin, Shanxi, eastern part of Inner Mongolia, Henan, Hubei, Hunan, Anhui and Jiangxi.

Agricultural and industrial output in the west differed widely from the rest of the country. In the early 1980s, only 14 percent of the agricultural and industrial output originated in the west as against 57 percent in the east and 29 percent in the central region. The investment in capital construction in the west also lagged behind other regions.

The per capita availability of arable land is 1.6 mu in the west. This does not appear unpromising in view of the overall availability in the country. But, lower cropping intensity came in the way of self-sufficiency in foodgrain in the western provinces. All the western provinces excepting Sichuan and Ningxia were deficient in foodgrain and average farm income in these provinces remained well below the national average.

The growth of rural industries in the east and the west varied enormously. In the early 1980s, the value of output in rural enterprises of eight eastern provinces *viz.*, Jiangsu, Zhejiang, Guangdong, Shandong, Liaoning, Beijing, Tianjin and Shanghai was thirteen times that of the eight western provinces *viz.*, Nei Monggol, Ningxia, Xianjiang, Gansu, Qinghai, Yunnan, Guizhou and Guangxi. In other words, of the total value of output in rural industries in these sixteen provinces, 93 percent was produced in the eight eastern provinces and 7 percent in the eight western provinces.

The shares of industrial and agricultural output of the abovementioned eight eastern provinces which are industrially developed and the eight western provinces which are industrially backward, are given in Table 5.4. This gives a precise idea about the disparity in the development process between the eastern and the western region.

Table 5.4: Output Shares in Eastern and Western Provinces

(Percentage)

	Eight Industrially Developed Provinces of the East	*Eight Industrially Backward Provinces of the West*	*East-West Differential*
1. Population	29.66 (70)	15.66 (63)	—
2. GAOV	34.50 (76)	12.60 (63)	1.45
3. Heavy Industry	49.30 (53)	8.70 (59)	2.99
4. Light Industry	56.70 (45)	6.50 (72)	4.61
5. GIOV	53.00 (44)	7.60 (57)	3.68
6. Foodgrain	29.40 (80)	12.70 (70)	1.22

Notes: 1. Eight industrially developed Eastern Provinces are: Jiangsu, Zhejiang, Guangdong, Shandong, Liaoning, Beijing, Tianjin and Shanghai.

2. Eight industrially backward Western Provinces are: Nei Monggol, Ningxia, Xianjiang, Gansu, Qinghai, Yunnan, Guizhou and Guangxi.

3. The figures in the brackets are coefficient of variation of the shares.

4. GAOV and GIOV are gross agricultural and industrial output value respectively.

The coefficient of variation of the output shares show that the inter-provincial disparity of the output shares of industry is more in the eight industrially backward western provinces. This is due to the setting up of some industries in a few western provinces, implying that the industries in this region did not develop uniformly among all the provinces, as in the eight eastern provinces. Because of the difference in population shares, which in the eight industrially developed eastern provinces is nearly twice of that of the eight industrially backward provinces of the west, it would not be proper to compare their output shares directly in order to figure out the disparity between these two groups of provinces. The difference in the shares, for this reason, has been computed after eliminating the differential shares of population between the industrially developed and backward regions, on a *pro-rata* basis. It shows that the share of industrial output in the industrially developed provinces is 3.7 times of that in the industrially backward provinces. The disparity is more in case of the output share of light industry, which is 4.6 times. The differential is less in case of agricultural output and foodgrain share.

Table 5.5: Correlation Matrix of Population and Output Shares in Eight Industrially Advanced and Eight Industrially Backward Provinces

I. Eight Eastern Provinces	*POPL*	*GAOV*	*HIND*	*LIND*	*GIOV*	*GRAIN*
POPL	1.00	0.95	0.05	0.15	0.05	0.97
GAOV		1.00	0.01	0.27	0.14	0.99
HIND			1.00	0.61	0.89	0.02
LIND				1.00	0.90	0.20
GIOV					1.00	0.10
GRAIN						1.00
II. Eight Western Provinces	POPL	GAOV	HIND	LIND	GIOV	GRAIN
POPL	1.00	0.95	0.56	0.89	0.85	0.95
GAOV		1.00	0.47	0.97	0.86	0.98
HIND			1.00	0.43	0.83	0.46
LIND				1.00	0.86	0.97
GIOV					1.00	0.86
GRAIN						1.00

Note: Legends are in Table 5.1

The correlation coefficient between the population and output shares of the eight industrially developed eastern provinces and the eight industrially backward western provinces are presented in Table 5.5. The correlation coefficient between population share and industrial output is low in the industrially developed provinces. It underlines the absence of association between the two, caused mainly by the high industrial output in provinces with low population share. In case of the industrially backward provinces, the correlation coefficient between the population and output shares are very high, indicating similarity in the output shares of agriculture and industry. The high correlation coefficient (greater than 0.95) between the population and output share of agriculture and foodgrain in both industrially developed and industrially backward provinces is the outcome of the policy of grain as a key link.

These disparities were mirrored in the average level of income and expenditure in the regions and ultimately in the level of living. It is not that the planners were unaware about the long-term consequences of the disparity between developed and underdeveloped regions. Their intention to disperse industrial growth is transparent in the acknowledgement of the need for construction of industrial base in the interior as early as in 1956.

But, exactly two decades later comes the admission of the failure in 1976 that the economic development of the west lagged far behind the east. The four provinces whose rate of economic growth in 1975-81 is least are from the west. The income of the province with highest per capita income in the west is one-fifth of that in the east.

The interstice between the west and the rest of the country stretched despite several attempts to integrate the economy of coastal region with the interior. The large-scale enterprises set up in the west failed to integrate into the local economy in the absence of smooth forward and backward linkages. The reduction in regional disparities, particularly in the standard of living, could have been better achieved through increasing agricultural productivity in backward areas and integrating rural areas with the rest of the economy through improved connectivity in terms of transport and communication. External trade could have been a possible route as the western provinces shared international border with as many as ten countries.

III
Urban-Rural Differential

The growth performance of urban and rural areas has been different, impacting on the disparity in the average income and consumption and also in the living standard between the two areas. The developing countries do not follow a uniform approach to demarcate the urban areas and as a consequence, the process and degree of urbanisation between the developing countries cease to be comparable. Agricultural operation has often been the general dividing line between rural and urban areas. The cities and towns are designated as urban areas and the people residing there as the urban population. Such an approach makes area and population mutually exclusive in the two areas, and their computation comparatively straightforward. But, the computation of urban population and the assessment of the nature and degree of urbanisation in China is rather complex due to mix-up of agricultural activity in the areas demarcated as town and city.

Urbanisation Process

There are two estimates of urban population in China. These are: (a) city and town population which include persons living in areas demarcated as cities and towns, (b) city and town non-agricultural population, where the persons engaged in agricultural activities in areas demarcated as cities and towns are excluded from the persons estimated in (a). The estimate of persons made in (b) is closer to the definition of urban population used in most developing countries. The urbanization rate, i.e., the percentage of urban population to total population for selected years during the period 1950-80 are given in Table 5.6. City and town population in China are 5 to 6 percent point more than non-agricultural population in towns.

Table 5.6: Urbanisation Rate: 1950-80

(Percentage)

No.	*Year*	*City and Town*	*City and Town Non-Agricultural*
1.	1955	15.2	13.5
2.	1960	24.7	19.7
3.	1965	18.0	13.6
4.	1970	17.4	12.4
5.	1980	19.5	13.7

Source: *Renkou Yu Jingji*, in Chinese, No. 6, 26 December 1985, Beijing, pp. 28-35.

The estimates of urban population are available from the three censuses conducted in 1953, 1964 and 1982. These estimates are not strictly comparable due to the changes in the criteria of demarcating areas as urban. The criteria adopted in the three censuses to demarcate areas as urban are:

(a) 1953 Census : areas with population 2500 or more, of which at least 50 percent of the work force engaged in non-agriculture.
(b) 1964 Census : areas with population 3000 or more, of which at least 70 percent of the work force engaged in non-agriculture.

(c) 1982 Census : areas with population between 2500 and 3000, of which at least 85 percent of the work force engaged in non-agriculture, and areas with population 3000 or more, of which at least 70 percent of the work force engaged in non-agriculture.

However, such differences, census-wise, are evident almost in all countries. China is no exception, and hence no correction has been made to account for the differences in the criteria and changes in the urban population over time have been measured from the census results. The growth of urban population in 1950-80 has been slow, by 2.6 percent or 3.8 percent per year depending on the definition used. These are lower than the annual growth of urban population of 4.3 percent experienced in developing countries during the same period. This slow pace of urbanization is the outcome of the statutory prohibition on migration from rural to urban areas, effected through household registration system and food rationing. As a part of the requirement of the plan, the movement of workers from villages to cities needed approval of the state. Even the transfer of workers from agriculture to commune industries required administrative sanction.

The restrictions on migration from rural to urban areas imposed right from the beginning, as early as 1952, contained the urban population. Yet, in the early 1980s, China's urban population was more than the total population of almost all the countries in the world. In spite of low growth, the change in population between 1950 and 1980 was sizable by virtue of a large base. The city and town population increased by 129.72 million and city and town non-agricultural population by 72.44 million in 1950-80. Thus, more than half (56 percent) of the increase in the city and town population was caused by increase in the city and town non-agricultural population.

The growth of urbanisation in 1950-80 can be decomposed into three stages. The first stage ensued the reconstruction phase with the installation of core industrial projects during the period 1950-55, which exemplified a steady and upward trend in urbanisation. The growth in urban population during this period was either 6 or 9 percent per year depending on the definition accepted.

The second stage of urbanisation is centered on the Great Leap Forward when the peasants migrated into city and town to join the industry. It increased the city and town population and non-agricultural population by 10 to 12 percent per year in 1955-60, and as a result, these two groups constituted 24.7 percent and 19.7 percent of the total population respectively in 1960. This is the highest ever rate of urbanisation attained in China under the central planning. However, this was a temporary phenomenon as the third stage (1961 to mid-1963) coincides with the reversion of urban population to the countryside in order to streamline the agriculture, which suffered serious setback during the Great Leap Forward. The flow of work force from the cities to the countryside during this period reduced the urban work force by 18.87 million and urban population by 26 million. The decline in the urbanisation rate persisted until 1970 when the city and town population and city and town non-agricultural population became 17.4 percent and 12.4 percent of the total population respectively.

Urbanisation is the outcome of natural growth and migration. The former in China remained relatively stable while the latter fluctuated over time in order to costume with the development strategy, an important facet of which is industrialisation and consequent creation of urban pockets in rural or uninhabited areas.

The census data of 1982 show considerable inter-provincial variation in the rate of urbanisation. It is high in the provinces in north-east and north-west and low to moderate in the east, central and south. The density of city and town is highest in the vicinity of Shanghai and least in Xizang and Qinghai.

The affiliation of the urbanisation rate to population density, a phenomenon to which the developing countries are universally familiar is evident in China with equal vigour. The density of urban conglomeration is observed to be associated positively with per capita industrial output and railway length.

The overall urban development centered on million-plus cities. Eleven of the twenty very large (population exceeding one million) and half of large cities (population between half a million and one million) are scattered along the east coast. In contrast, 15 of the 29 provinces are not touched by a single very large city and nine do not have a large city. The large and very large cities are political, economic and cultural centres. Industrial centre and educational and scientific research institutions are generally located in the city. The socio-economic changes in a society are to a great extent related to the degree of urbanisation and indeed, a developed and modernised economy is more related to the urban sector than to the rural.

Income and Consumption

The urban-rural differential in per capita income and consumption and in availability of public services are assessed in order to compare the material aspects of the level of living of the peasants in the rural environment with that of the workers in the cities.

At the national level, average wage of workers and staff in urban areas is 9.3 times of the income of workers and peasants in commune. In as many as eleven provinces covering two-fifth of total population, the average wages of workers and staff in urban areas exceed that of commune income by at least ten times. This disparity is particularly high in the underdeveloped areas such as Gansu and Guizhou, where it is about fifteen times, and low in the sub-urban areas of Beijing, Shanghai and Tianjin.[2] The income of commune members do not fully represent rural income as it is usually supplemented by earnings from private land and subsidiary occupation. Hence, it may marginally overstate the urban rural income differential computed above. The wide inter-provincial disparity in the income of these two groups originate from the differential productivity in agriculture and industry.

The per capita expenditure of the peasants and the non-agricultural population given in Table 5.7 can also be used to express urban-rural differential. Per capita expenditure of the non-agricultural population in nominal terms is twice of that of the peasants and this remained unchanged between 1952 and 1975.

The price rise of the consumption basket of the peasants and non-agricultural population was similar until 1957. Thereafter, the prices of goods that constitute the consumption basket of the peasants increased faster than that of the non-agricultural population. Between 1957 and 1975, it increased by 1.4 percent annually for peasants as against 0.6 percent annually for non-agricultural population. The prices of commodities that constitute the consumption basket of peasants rose faster than those of non-agricultural population in years of low economic growth whereas the two prices moved closely in a regime of high growth, clearly marking an urban bias.

Table 5.7: Expenditure of Peasants and Non-Agricultural Population (at current prices)

(Yuan, per capita, yearly)

		1952		*1957*		*1975*	
1.	Peasant	62	(100.0)	79	(117.1)	124	(143.1)
2.	Non-Agricultural Population	148	(100.0)	205	(126.3)	324	(181.1)
	Total	76	(100.0)	102	(122.9)	158	(156.9)

Note: The figures in brackets are index of per capita real consumption.

Source: 1. *Statistical Year Book of China,* State Statistical Bureau, Beijing, 1981. pp. 435-36.

2. *Economic Adjustment and Reform,* Special Feature Series, Beijing Review, Beijing, 1982, Table 5, p. 218.
3. Liang Wensen, "Balanced Development of Industry and Agriculture", in Xu Dixin, *China's Search for Economic Growth,* Beijing, 1982, p. 55.

Table 5.8 gives the growth in per capita consumption expenditure of the peasants and the non-agricultural population in real terms. The rate of growth of per capita consumption of the two groups differs, particularly after 1957, which is a period of low economic growth. In developing countries, the rural areas are generally the worst victims of reduction in the rate of economic growth. China is no exception despite the household registration system, which prevented some of the rural work force to enter into urban areas, and the food rationing, which tied the rural people to their native place. Internal migration could have developed the urban services sector and reduced the disparity in income and consumption between rural and urban areas. The statutory control on internal migration, both between rural and urban areas, and within each area, only aggravated the disparity.

Table 5.8: Growth in Expenditure of Peasants and Non-Agricultural Population

(percent per year)

Period	*Peasant*	*Non-Agricultural Population*	*Total*
1. 1952 to 1957	3.2	4.8	4.2
2. 1957 to 1975	1.1	2.0	1.4
3. 1952 to 1975	1.6	2.6	2.0

The per capita consumption in rural and urban areas summarily brings into surface the following:

(a) Both average consumption expenditure and its rate of growth in urban areas are more than rural.
(b) Cost of consumption basket in rural areas increased faster than urban, particularly in years of low economic growth.
(c) In years of low economic growth, both urban-rural price differential and urban-rural disparity in per capita consumption becomes more.
(d) High economic growth has a sobering effect on the per capita consumption differential.
(e) In years of low economic growth, the State through subsidy and other measures protected urban consumption more than rural.

The urban-rural disparity is profound in the consumption of essential items, both of food and non-food, given in Table 5.9. In 1978, per capita consumption in urban areas was three times of that in rural. Per capita monthly cereal consumption in urban areas was two jin (one kilogram) more than rural. Besides, the quality of food in rural areas is generally poor. The consumption of oil, sugar and blended cloth in urban areas is 3 to 4 times of rural. An average urbanite uses five and a half times of coal than rural. Soap is indeed a luxury for rural inhabitants as each uses less than two soap cakes in one full year, as against 15 soap cakes in urban. The differential is lower in cotton cloth, beef and mutton, between two and three times. The consumption of these items is too low to be more unequal. For example, the monthly per capita consumption of beef and mutton is as low as 97 grams in urban areas and 54 grams in rural. The increase in the availability of a product has invariably been accompanied by increase in its urban-rural differential.

Table 5.9: Consumption of Basic Necessities in 1978

(jin, per capita, yearly)

No.	*Item*	*Total*	*Urban*	*Rural*	*Urban/Rural*
1.	Cereal	390.92	410.58	386.66	1.1
2.	Vegetable Oil	3.19	8.21	2.10	3.9
3.	Pork	15.34	27.39	12.73	2.1
4.	Beef and Mutton	1.50	2.36	1.31	1.8
5.	Poultry	0.87	1.79	0.67	2.7
6.	Aquatic Products	7.00	17.68	4.68	3.8
7.	Sugar	6.84	16.29	4.79	3.4
8.	Cotton Cloth (chi)	19.97	31.32	17.51	1.8
9.	Blended Cloth (chi)	4.14	11.61	2.52	4.6
10.	Wool (chi)	0.25	0.80	0.14	5.7
11.	Shoes (pair)	0.91	1.99	0.67	3.0
12.	Soap (cakes)	4.02	14.71	1.70	8.7
13.	Coal	210.31	642.74	116.57	5.5
14.	Per Capita Yearly Consumption (Yuan)	175	383	132	2.9

Source: Tongji, No. 8, 17 August, 1985, pp. 47-48, Beijing.

The urban bias in income generation has left its stamp on the ownership of consumer durables also. In 1978, there were 233 bicycles and 202 radio sets per thousand persons in urban areas as against 43 and 51 respectively in rural. Similar difference exists in case of sewing machine, wristwatches, etc.

City *vs.* Countryside

The pattern of industrial development did not create favourable condition for industrial dispersal, essential to reduce the disparity between the city and the countryside. Industrial development bypassed the countryside and was concentrated in large and medium sized cities. In 1980, the cities accounted for 18.5 percent of total population. But, it generated 69 percent of industrial output, 75.5 percent of the output in state owned industries, 65.2 percent of the output of light industry, 49.5 percent of industrial output in collective owned units and 67.4 percent of industrial fixed assets. The cities account for 91.4 percent of total employment generation in various joint enterprises in industry, 55.6 percent of total employment of staff and workers in collective owned units, 67.9 percent of employment of staff and workers in industrial enterprises and 56.9 percent in state owned industries.

The spatial distribution of public services is also skewed in favour of the cities. The cities account for (a) 94.9 percent of the students in institutions of higher learning, (b) 68 percent of the students in secondary schools, and (c) 71.5 percent of the students in workers training schools. Half of the medical personnel and health workers are rooted in the city. About two-fifth of all beds in health centres and hospitals are located in the city. Besides, the quality of such service is generally poor in the countryside, as the efficient personnel would always like to flock around the city for the cause of professional excellence. The scientific and technical institutes are mostly located in the cities.

The disparity in per person availability of a service between city and the countryside can be quantified from the ratio $[Q(1-P)]/[P(1-Q)]$ where, P and Q are the city's share in population and the variable. The disparities are: (a) per person industrial employment in cities is 80 percent more than the countryside, (b) in state owned units, per person output in cities is 13.6 times of that in the countryside, and (c) industrial output, both light and heavy industries and fixed asset, by 8 to 10 times.

A more skewed picture is vivid from the socio-economic indicators of 266 large and small cities.[3] These cities account for one-tenth of the country's population but two-third of the total employment in industrial enterprises and value of fixed assets. This one-tenth of the population also account for 84.6 percent of the industrial output and as a consequence, is responsible for 85.3 percent of profit and tax. The ability to pay tax being one of the principal yardsticks of well-being underline the city-orientation of the development process.

These differences between city and countryside no doubt is the outcome of the various state policies, the important of which is the policy of restricting internal migration through the household registration system. The status of urban residents remained at an elevated level compared to the rural folks. The life in the cities of China had a distinctive character, different in many ways from the cities in developing countries.

The Disparity : Why and How

Per capita consumption of all population increased by 77 percent in 1952-78. The increase is 57.5 percent for agricultural and 112.9 percent for non-agricultural population. The difference in net income between the agricultural and the non-agricultural population would be higher as foodgrain assistance, state grant and other benefits are based progressively on personal income. The financial subsidy accrued more to urban areas. In 1982, per capita financial subsidy in urban areas was six and a half times of that in rural. It was 95.81 Yuan in urban and 14.73 Yuan in rural.[4] Such high subsidization of the real income of urbanites nevertheless was aimed to contain social unrest, a widely observable feature in most developing countries.

The economic and cultural astern of the countryside is caused by poor educational standard and health care facilities in rural areas. The growth differential in agriculture and industry lies at the root of urban-rural disparity in income and level of living. Industrial growth is not sufficiently oriented to meet the exigencies of agriculture. In the absence of adequate investment in agriculture, the disparity-reducing impact of agricultural growth receded.

The development process in the initial stages cause rural to urban flow of funds and technical manpower, which in general, is backed up by a return flow. Under its influence rural-urban income gap tends to widen at the initial stages of development only to be closed later. Rural to urban flow did take place in China but the impact of the reverse flow was ephemeral. Increase in agricultural productivity, reduction in dependence on land and diversification of rural economic structure are the principal means to narrow the rural-urban income gap. These issues though are of great significance in the formulation of a sound development strategy, were not addressed properly and the urban-rural gap in income and consequently, in the level of living and quality of life, remained insurmountable.

REFERENCES

1. Feng Shixin, *Jingji Kexue,* No. 3, 20 June 1985, pp. 52-55, Beijing.
2. A *Zhonggue Baike Nianjian,* July, 1981, p. 70.
3. Li Mengbai, *Guangzhou Yangiu,* No. 4, April 1986, pp. 4-9, Guangzhou.
4. Zhang Tong, *Nongye Jingji Wenti,* No. 7, 23 February 1984, pp. 37-40, Beijing; He Kang and Sun Xiang, *Renmin Ribao,* 8 July 1980, p. 5, Beijing.

6

Economic Reforms

For a quarter century, China was a victim of central planning. The major macro-and socio-economic variables that determine the levels of living and quality of life stagnated in the central plan era (1952-78), forcing them to reform the economic system and embrace market economy, the center piece of development strategy of the capitalist world. This chapter deals with the policies and programmes pursued under economic reforms and their outcome during China's tryst with market mechanism.

I
The Preamble

The idea of reforming the economic system was mooted in the Third Plenum of the National Party Congress's Eleventh Central Committee held in December 1978. It meant dismantling of the central planning apparatus and putting in place a market based economic structure - a complex task for a country as vast as China.

Under central planning, the State controlled the means of production and distribution and directly participated in every economic activity. The agricultural production was managed by the commune organization. The farmers as members of commune were engaged in agriculture and their income depended almost entirely on agricultural production. The policy of "grain as a key link" prevented the farmers to embark on allied activities of agriculture and even to cultivation of commercial crops before meeting the target of grain production. The industries were owned and managed by the state. Most of the industries became inefficient and suffered losses, resulting in mounting state subsidy. Service sector was considered unproductive and hence neglected. The monetary and fiscal variables were dictated by the state and hence treated as exogenous in the system. The banking system was virtually a surrogate of the Finance Ministry. The taxes collected by the provincial governments were deposited with the central government. The central government in turn, allocated resources to the provincial governments according to their requirements. The central government enjoyed immense power in the area of resource mobilization and expenditure. The provinces generally had to implement the policies and programmes framed by the central government.

The reform of the economic system began with relaxation of state control on economic activity and ensuring a role for market and private sector, both of which were non-existent under central planning. An entrepreneurial class based on private initiative surfaced, initially in agriculture and then in industries and services sectors. In agriculture, the responsibility system acted as an incentive to production and by mid-1980s there was enough production of both grain and non-grain. The allied activities of agriculture became diversified, resulting in a balanced development of agriculture. The state owned industries were granted autonomy in management. Some of them were privatized. In conformity, the source of industrial investment changed from state exchequer to loans and borrowing from money and capital market. The destination of investment switched from state sector to private and joint state-private sector. The activities in services sector expanded. Adequate incentive and protection to the private sector was granted by the Constitution.

The fiscal and monetary variables came to be increasingly market determined. In fiscal areas, the tax reform granted more authority to the provincial and local governments and made the devolution of taxes from central to provincial governments transparent. The banking system was freed from Ministerial control and made sensitive to market needs. The commercial banks began to operate on commercial lines, being responsible for their financial performance. Prices began to reflect the cost of production and set in the market. It was increasingly being used as an instrument to equate demand and supply. The commodities and services covered by state administered prices reduced and so also price subsidy. Since the prevailing laws of the land did not permit implementation of most of the abovementioned reform policies, a new Constitution was adopted in December, 1982 to provide the required statutory back-up.[1] The 1982 Constitution was amended twice, in April 1988 and March 1993 in order to re-define the role of the state in economic planning and market regulation, considered essential to ensure the material progress of the nation.

The manner of implementation of economic reforms in China was different from most developing countries. The developing countries, which were practicing some form of planning earlier, pursued the reform programmes throughout the country simultaneously. In contrast, China decided to undertake a program of "gradual but fundamental" reform of its economy. The reform programmes were initially applied in selected areas and then based upon the results a view was taken about its extension to the national level.

The Chinese economy in 2000 cannot be called a market economy though it ceases to be a centrally planned economy. The state and the private sector co-exist in an environment where the private sector operates under the guidance and direction laid down by the state. This resembles to mixed economy, a notable example being its neighbour, India. The state remains responsible for planning and development of the economy. The national economic plan is formulated by the state council (equivalent to cabinet in Western democracies), which is the highest organ of state administration. The state council is also responsible for preparing the state budget, through which the national economic plan is implemented.

II
Macro-Economic Scenario

The economic reform transformed the macro-economic scenario. The annual average growth rates of Gross Domestic Product (a summary measure of income) in real terms (comparable or constant prices) are given in Table 6.1. The overall rate of economic growth during the reform period (1978-2000) works out to 9.5 per cent per year. Driven by services sector, the GDP in tertiary sector increased by 12.26 per cent per year in the 1980s. The growth of secondary sector by 17.38 per cent per year in 1990-95 can be associated with the industrial reform carried out in this period. The realized growth rate is far greater than that achieved by the former centrally planned economies of Eastern Europe, known as transition economies and also of the former Soviet economies despite the assistance the latter received from the developed capitalist world.

A word of caution on the accuracy of the GDP growth rates during the reform period estimated from the Chinese official statistics may perhaps be in order. Studies made by international organizations such as the World Bank and the Organization for Economic Cooperation and Development (OECD), and national organization such as the National Economic Research Center (of China), have demonstrated varying degrees of overestimation in the GDP growth rates measured from official statistics. According to a World Bank estimate, the long-term growth between 1978 and 1995 overstates real growth by 1.2 percentage points per year. Dividing the period 1978-95 into two sub-periods, 1978-86 and 1986-95, the World Bank estimates point out that the overestimation more than tripled between the first (1978-86) and the second sub-period (1986-95). The estimates made by OECD in this regard are wider than the World Bank. It places the growth rate for the period 1986-94 as 3.8 percentage point lower than the estimates made from official statistics. Within the country, China's National Economic Research Center, after an extensive research work, calculated the growth rate for the period 1978-98 as 8.4 percent per year, which is also below the official estimate of 9.7 percent per year. [2]

Table 6.1: Growth Rates of GDP

(percent per year, compound)

Period	*Primary*	*Secondary*	*Tertiary*	*Total*
1. 1978 to 1985	6.50	10.24	12.76	9.84
2. 1985 to 1990	4.18	8.97	9.38	7.87
3. 1990 to 1995	4.15	17.38	9.95	12.00
4. 1995 to 2000	3.46	9.84	8.17	8.27
5. 1980 to 1990	6.19	9.48	12.26	9.28
6. 1990 to 2000	3.80	13.55	9.06	10.12
7. 1978 to 2000	4.74	11.44	10.30	9.51

Despite these reservations on the official data, there appears to be little doubt that China did achieve high rate of growth over this period. The high growth rate impacted on the structure of the economy by way of reduced dependence of income generation on the primary sector. The average sectoral shares of GDP given in Table 6.2 embody the structural shift. From this, the growth and development in the reform period can be compartmentalized into three phases as (a) 1980 to 1984 (b) 1985 to 1992 and (c) 1993 to 2000. The income generation in primary sector declined in a secular fashion in all the three phases and the magnitude of decline from one phase to the other is near equal. The transition from first (1980-84) to second phase (1985-92) is dominated by the increase in income share of tertiary sector. The increase income of secondary sector dominates the transition from second (1985-92) to third phase (1993-2000).

Table 6.2: Structure of GDP

(Percentage)

Average for the Period	*Primary*	*Secondary*	*Tertiary*
1. 1980 to 1984	32.0	45.6	22.4
2. 1985 to 1992	25.8	43.2	31.0
3. 1993 to 2000	19.0	49.2	31.8

The realization of high growth rate and structural change in the economy were achieved with an optimum ratio of consumption and investment. The choice between consumption and investment rate in the central plan era created distortion in macro-economic balance; its prime victim was the rate of economic growth. The consumption and investment rates were changed during the reform period, but in costume with the exigencies, and not beyond a point where it threatens sectoral balance. The average consumption and investment rates in the reform era given in Table 6.3 show that the change was confined to five percentage point with a stable share of household consumption in total consumption. Consumption and investment rates since 1978 are given in Annexure A.1.

Table 6.3: Consumption and Investment Rates

Indicator/Year	*1978 -85*	*1986 -92*	*1993-2000*	*1999-2000*	*1978-2000*
1. As per cent of GDP					
a) Household Consumption	51.5	49.9	46.8	47.9	47.6
b) Government Consumption	14.0	12.8	12.2	12.9	12.5
c) Total Consumption	65.5	62.7	59.0	60.8	60.1
d) Investment	35.0	36.6	38.6	36.7	38.0
2. As Per cent of Consumption					
a) Household Consumption	78.6	79.6	79.3	78.8	79.2
b) Government Consumption	21.4	20.4	20.7	21.2	20.8

Note: The rates are calculated at current prices. The consumption and investment rates do not add up to 100 as net export is added to GDP.

The nature of growth in the reform period can be traced from the movement of the medium term growth rates, estimated for primary, secondary and tertiary sector GDP, treating eight year as the medium term (not so arbitrary in view of the length of reform period as 22 years). The annual average growth rates for the medium term and the regression parameters of the linear time trend of the growth rates are given in Table 6.4. Indices of real GDP by sectors and its composition since 1978 are given in Annexure-A.2.

The regression coefficients of the linear time trend of the medium term growth rates indicate acceleration of growth rate of GDP in secondary sector during the reform period (1978-2000). The growth rate of total GDP shows signs of acceleration over the period 1982-1999. The growth rates of primary and tertiary sector decelerated as the high growth rates in the initial years of reform mainly arising from pent-up demand was not sustainable in the long run. For primary sector, the deceleration was at a lower growth rate insinuated by the structural change in the economy.

China in 1978 was categorized by the World Bank as a low-income economy. The high growth in GDP during the reform period propelled it to the lower middle-income group in the later half of the 1990s. Throughout the 1980s and 1990s, the rates of economic growth in China, both aggregate and sectoral, were far greater than those of low and middle income countries.[3] In order to place the acceleration of the rate of growth of the Chinese economy in a broader perspective, it may be useful to compare its performance with those of broad categories of countries over the same period. Table 6.5 gives a comparison of the annual growth rates of the economies in low and middle income countries and China in the 1980s and 1990s.

Table 6.4: Medium Term Growth Rates of GDP

(per cent per year, compound)

Period	*Primary Sector*	*Secondary Sector*	*Tertiary Sector*	*Total GDP*
1. 1978 to 1986	6.09	10.24	12.69	9.72
2. 1979 to 1987	5.92	10.93	13.52	10.22
3. 1980 to 1988	6.44	11.04	14.47	10.65
4. 1981 to 1989	5.94	11.30	13.79	10.49
5. 1982 to 1990	5.44	10.98	12.39	9.82
6. 1983 to 1991	4.71	11.42	11.59	9.61
7. 1984 to 1992	3.72	12.21	10.75	9.50
8. 1985 to 1993	4.08	12.36	9.84	9.50
9. 1986 to 1994	4.17	13.36	9.52	9.97
10. 1987 to 1995	4.20	13.38	8.79	9.84
11. 1988 to 1996	4.53	13.08	8.13	9.63
12. 1989 to 1997	4.58	13.97	8.61	10.24
13. 1990 to 1998	4.10	14.75	9.39	10.77
14. 1991 to 1999	4.16	14.01	9.25	10.51
15. 1992 to 2000	3.87	12.60	8.68	9.73
Linear Time Trend:				
a) Regression Coefficient	-0.1660 (5.1)	0.2699 (7.0)	-0.4266 (7.1)	0.1105 (3.4)
b) R-bar Square	0.64	0.77	0.78	0.54

Note: 1. The linear time trend of growth rates are estimated for the period 1978 to 2000 except for Total GDP for which it is estimated for 1982 to 1999.

2. The figures in brackets are t-values.

Table 6.5: Growth of Economies

(*percent, per year*)

Item	*1980-90*	*1980-90*	*1980-90*	*1980-90*	*1980-90*	*1990-99*	*1990-99*	*1990-99*	*1990-99*	*1990-99*
	China	*LI*	*LMI*	*UMI*	*MI*	*China*	*LI*	*LMI*	*UMI*	*MI*
1. Agriculture	5.9	3.0	4.0	2.8	3.5	4.3	2.5	2.0	1.9	2.0
2. Industry	11.1	5.4	4.1	2.3	3.6	14.4	1.1	5.2	3.9	4.4
3. Services	13.5	5.7	5.3	2.8	3.5	9.2	4.7	3.7	3.6	3.6
4. Total: GDP at Factor Cost	10.1	4.4	4.0	2.5	3.2	10.7	2.4	3.4	3.6	3.5

Legend: LI = Low Income Countries, LMI = Lower Middle Income Countries, UMI = Upper Income Countries, MI = Middle Income Countries.

Source: World Bank Estimates.

III
Income, Consumption and Poverty

The high rate of economic growth was translated into increase in per capita income and consumption of rural and urban households as can be observed from Table 6.6. Mainly as a result of the re-structuring of agriculture, the rate of increase in per capita income and consumption in rural areas in the initial years of reform (1978-85) was more than that in urban. Thereafter, the increases were more in urban areas than in rural. These increases in the per capita income and consumption were reflected in the increase in consumption of essential items, besides foodgrain, and ultimately in the improvement in standard of living. The impact of the increase in income and consumption was also evident in the reduced number of people living in absolute poverty.

Table 6.6: Growth Rates of Per Capita Income and Consumption

(percent per year, compound)

Period	*Income Rural*	*Income Urban*	*Consumption Rural*	*Consumption Urban*
1. 1978 to 1985	15.18	6.98	9.96	5.71
2. 1985 to 1990	2.97	4.31	2.46	6.08
3. 1990 to 1995	4.28	7.94	7.06	7.89
4. 1995 to 2000	4.73	5.74	5.86*	6.32*
5. 1980 to 1990	8.39	4.55	6.63	5.88
6. 1990 to 2000	4.50	6.83	6.52#	7.19 #
7. 1978 to 2000	7.43	6.30	6.66 @	6.43 @

* relate to 1995 to 1999; # relate to 1990 to 1999; @ relate to 1978 to 1999

The income growth in rural areas did not affect the personal income distribution much.[4] The gains in policy changes in agriculture brought about increase in income and consumption of the farmers across the board. The pattern of income distribution that emerged, yielded a three-fold increase in the percentage of rural households with annual per capita income of more than 500

Yuan in a span of 15 years (from 22.17 per cent in 1985 to 65.29 per cent in 2000) as can be seen from the distribution of rural households by per capita income given in Table 6.7.[5] The percentage of households with annual per capita income more than 1000 Yuan increased from 2.2 per cent in 1985 to 23.17 per cent in 2000. These increases are real since the income group wise percentage of persons are worked out after eliminating the price inflation.

Table 6.7: Distribution of Rural Households by Per Capita Income

(Percentage)

Expenditure Limit (Yuan, per capita, yearly) Real at 1985 Prices	*1985 (100.0)*	*1990 (165.1)*	*1995 (291.4)*	*2000 (314.0)*
1. 0 to 200	12.15	12.25	5.12	4.63
2. 200 to 500	65.68	59.10	49.54	30.08
3. 500 to 1000	19.97	24.22	34.44	42.12
4. 1000 +	2.20	4.43	10.90	23.17
Total	100.00	100.00	100.00	100.00

Note: The figures in brackets in the top row are general consumer price indices in rural areas, used to convert the nominal expenditure distribution to real.

The nature of movement of per capita income of rural and urban population during economic reforms has been assessed from their medium term growth rates, treating eight year as the medium term as in the case of GDP. The annual average growth rates and their linear time trend are given in Table 6.8. Yearly per capita consumption and net income since 1978 are given in Annexure A.3.

The regression coefficient of the linear time trend of medium term growth rates indicate acceleration in the growth rate of per capita urban income and deceleration in the growth of per capita rural income. The latter is due to the high income growth realized in the initial years of reform. The medium term growth rate of per capita rural income remains above 10 per cent until 1988. Such high growth rate is difficult to sustain over the long run and hence the deceleration.

Table 6.8: Medium Term Growth Rates of Per Capita Income

(per cent per year, compound)

	Period	*Rural*	*Urban*
1.	1978 to 1986	13.61	7.81
2.	1979 to 1987	11.85	6.53
3.	1980 to 1988	10.58	4.64
4.	1981 to 1989	8.40	4.60
5.	1982 to 1990	6.20	5.02
6.	1983 to 1991	4.71	5.29
7.	1984 to 1992	3.80	4.96
8.	1985 to 1993	3.23	5.97
9.	1986 to 1994	3.46	5.34
10.	1987 to 1995	3.47	5.66
11.	1988 to 1996	3.78	6.48
12.	1989 to 1997	4.58	6.91
13.	1990 to 1998	4.90	6.58
14.	1991 to 1999	5.13	6.84
15.	1992 to 2000	4.65	6.44
Linear Time Trend:			
a)	Regression Coefficient	-0.5601 (4.1)	0.1971 (7.7)
b)	R-bar Square	0.53	0.83

Note: 1. The linear time trend of growth rates are estimated for the period 1978 to 2000 for rural income and for 1980 to 2000 for urban income.
2. The figures in brackets are t-values.

The increase in income and consumption and the overall improvement in living standard is reflected in reduced household size and in number of persons supported by each employee. Table 6.9 shows: (a) the household size in China is lower than in other developing countries, (b) the household size in rural areas is more than in urban areas, (c) the household size in both rural and urban areas declined after 1985 and (d) the number of persons supported by each employee declined in the rural areas but increased in the urban areas.

Table 6.9: Household Size and Persons Supported by Employee

Item	*1985 Rural*	*1985 Urban*	*1990 Rural*	*1900 Urban*	*1995 Rural*	*1995 Urban*	*2000 Rural*	*2000 Urban*
1. Household Size	—	3.89	4.80	3.50	4.48	3.23	4.20	3.13
2. Persons Supported by Each Employee*	1.74	1.81	1.64	1.77	1.56	1.73	1.52	1.86

Note: Estimated from the Survey data.

* including the employee.

The distribution corrected growth rate of per capita private consumption for 30 low-income countries, 25 lower middle income countries, 11 upper middle income countries and 21 high income countries are available from the World Bank.[6] The distribution corrected growth rates indicate more efficiently the impact of private consumption on poverty reduction. Ravallion and Chen have shown that rate of poverty reduction is on the average proportional to distribution corrected growth of private consumption. [7] The annual average growth of distribution corrected per capita private consumption in China is 4.3 per cent per year for the period 1980 to 1998, next only to 4.4 per cent per year of Korea Republic.

The sample survey data on income and consumption, gathered at the household level indicate sharp reduction in the number of rural poor between 1978, i.e., the year in which central planning was abandoned and 1985, i.e., by the time Responsibility System in agriculture was extended to the entire rural areas of the country. According to official estimates, the number of persons living below the poverty line in the rural areas reduced from 250 million in 1978 to 125 million in 1985. Although there are disputes about the estimates of the level and reduction of poverty in China arising mainly from the conceptualization of the poverty line and comparability of the household level data on consumption and income, both spatial and inter-temporal, there appears to be some degree of consensus about the number of people being lifted out of poverty during the reform period. Between 1978 and 2000, about 230 million Chinese have been lifted out of absolute poverty – a remarkable feat particularly in view of the contrasting scenario in the developing countries where 100 million persons joined the poverty group during this period.[8] The income distribution in rural and urban areas might have worsened in the 1990s due to uneven distribution of the benefits of growth, but economic growth was high enough to outstrip the adverse impact of the rise in income inequality.

IV
Agriculture

The reform in agriculture began with an experiment with private initiative in which the commune relegated its authority on agricultural land by leasing it to groups of peasants. A contract was signed between the peasants and the state (represented by the commune) in which the peasants took the responsibility of providing a fixed amount of output to the state in lieu of the use of land. The peasants retained the excess production for either sale in the rural market or for self-consumption. The sale of the excess production in the market was no longer a losing proposition because farm prices were raised as a result of the price reform. The procurement price of farm products was raised by 22 per cent in 1979 alone. Perhaps as the peasants were responsible for production, this method of contracting farm output in the commune land came to be known as Responsibility System.

The Responsibility System was initially applied to production of foodgrain in selected areas. The areas were chosen after detail deliberations. First, a few provinces were chosen where it was expected to produce favourable result. Within these provinces, a few communes were chosen to experiment this system from various angles. Finally, some areas were earmarked within the communes. The experiment with the Responsibility System began in 1979. Its success in raising agricultural production and farmers' income was phenomenal and instant. Yet, it was extended to other areas gradually. By 1984, 98 per cent of the production teams adopted the Responsibility System. In the absence of its major work, viz., management of agricultural production, the commune organization was abolished. Some new organizations were created and old ones revived to transfer the remaining responsibilities of the commune. The law and order and management of the commune and brigade enterprises were placed with the Township and Town Governments, which was the level of administration in the pre-commune era. Most of the responsibilities of the production teams were entrusted to Village Committees. The Village Committees were not formal government institutions but assisted the Township and Town governments in the maintenance of law and order and managed some social services. In 1985, there were 91 thousand Township and Town Governments and 940.6 thousand Village Committees. These were subsequently re-organized. In 2000, there were 735 thousand Village Committees and 43735 Township and Town Governments, of which 19692 were Town Governments.

The policy of "grain as a key link", one of the fundamental tenets of central planning under which the rural population were tied to their native soil and kept engaged in agriculture, gave way to production decisions based on comparative advantage of the regions. This not only raised the output of food and commercial crops but also opened up avenues for allied activities of agriculture. A class of rural households exploited the potentials of animal husbandry and agro-based industries and came to be known as specialized households. Besides directly engaged in the production of goods and services, they participated in entrepreneurial activities. The average income of the specialized households was far in excess of the farmers and a few of them became enviably wealthy by the standard then prevailing in rural areas.

The increase in agricultural production and rural income through the Responsibility System and emergence of specialized households are the visible gains of reform. Per capita grain output in the central plan regime stagnated. In the reform period, it increased from 329.4 kg in 1978-80 to 406.5 kg in 1997-99, implying a growth rate of 1.1 percent per year for nearly two decades. The output of oil bearing crops stagnated in the central plan era as farmers were not allowed to cultivate these before fulfilling the target of grain production. Per capita output of oil bearing crops in 2000 was 4.3 times as compared to 1978. Its growth occurred in two phases, by 14.5 per cent per year in 1978-1985 and by 6.3 per cent per year in 1992-2000.

The increase in agricultural output was reflected on rural income. In 1980, only 1.6 per cent of the rural households earned between 500 Yuan and 2000 Yuan per year. The income of 22.2 per cent of the households fell in this range in 1985. The source of rural income changed. In 1978, two-third of the net income of farmers originated from collectives; within four years of reform it reduced to about one-fifth. In 1985, more than 80 per cent of the income of the farm families originated from household activities. The origin of rural income given in Table 6.10 shows that about half of the income originated in farming until the mid-1990s. This reduced to about one-third in 2000.

Table 6.10: Origin of Rural Income

(Percentage)

	1985	*1990*	*1995*	*2000*
I. By Source				
1. Wages	18.15	20.22	22.42	31.17
2. Household Activities	74.44	75.56	71.35	63.34
a) Farming	50.82	50.21	50.67	37.01
b) Others*	23.62	25.35	20.68	26.33
3. Transfer and Property Income	7.41	4.22	6.23	5.49
II. By Economic Activity				
1. Productive	92.48	95.78	93.77	94.50
a) Primary Sector	75.02	74.43	63.16	50.41
b) Secondary Sector	7.41	10.30	18.20	26.55
c) Tertiary Sector	10.05	11.05	12.41	17.54
2. Non-Productive	7.52	4.22	6.23	5.50

* Others include animal husbandry, forestry, fishery, trade, transport services.

The income generation by type of economic activity changed. Primary sector generated three-fourth of rural income in 1985; it reduced to half in 2000. The role of secondary sector in rural income generation increased. The dependence of rural work force on agriculture reduced. From 1978 to 2000, the proportion of work force employed in agriculture reduced from 70 per cent to 50 per cent while that in tertiary sector increased from 12.2 per cent to 27.5 per cent.

The invisible gain of reform is the private initiative in agriculture where the peasants shared the investment, applied modern technology and inputs, rather than being dependent on the state. Private capital in the rural areas was allowed to flow across administrative boundaries. The specialized households seized this opportunity and expanded their activities in non-agricultural areas outside their own village.

In China, the value added per worker in agriculture sector increased by 3.2 per cent per year from 1979-81 to 1996-98, and that of food production index by 5.9 per cent per year. These are no mean achievements when compared with the performance of the low income and lower middle-income countries where the value added in agriculture during the same period increased by 2.8 per cent per year and 3.1 per cent per year respectively and that of food production index increased by 3.32 per cent per year and 4.65 per cent per year respectively.[9]

The policy measures in agriculture though made considerable impact by way of reducing the level of poverty and deprivation among the rural population, a group emerged as vulnerable who were earlier protected by food ration from the commune organization. In the reform period, they were assisted by poverty alleviation programmes. These programmes were subsequently broad-based with additional investment in agricultural and non-agricultural enterprises in the poor areas, and further to area development approach in which the poorest of the poor counties were assisted with special investment program. Such anti-poverty programmes, aimed to increase the income of the poor directly, bypassing the general growth process, are known for their efficacy of reducing the level of poverty and containing income inequality.

The reform in agriculture manifests the state's concern for increased production and control over the peasants. The state exercised its control through the terms and conditions of the contract under the Responsibility System which varied over space in order to comply with the regional agricultural practices. The peasants were bound to cultivate the crop for which the contract was signed and sub-contracting of production was not allowed. The state control on the peasants and agriculture was also effected through the ownership of land. The land was a collective property and belonged to the state. The land in rural and sub-urban areas, including the house sites and privately farmed plots of cropland and hilly land are owned by the collectives. The land in cities are owned by the state. The agricultural land are leased to the peasants for the period of the contract. The economic reforms do not confer peasants with the ownership rights of land.

V
Industry

The development debate in the central plan era focused on whether egalitarianism should prevail over material progress of the nation, that is, whether equity should be preferred to growth in income. The essentiality of industrialization and modernization was debated on the extent to which the country should adopt the latest technology. The development of a modern industrial sector was not possible without compromising with the reigning socialist principles, particularly the egalitarian policies. The issue during the reform period boiled down to the level of income inequality that the country can afford to tolerate in the course of development; a classic case of growth-equity trade-off. This trade-off made the reform of industrial sector somewhat slower, and perhaps complicated though a cluster of policies were formulated to free the industrial sector from direct state interference, and implemented in a step-by-step approach, heralding the entry of private sector in industrial development and greater autonomy for state-owned industries.

The industries in the central planning era were categorized into two groups in terms of their ownership structure. These are: (a) ownership of the whole people and (b) collective ownership of the working people, commonly known as collective ownership. The large state owned industries located in the urban areas and managed by the central or provincial governments or cities with independent planning status were covered under the ownership of the whole people. The smaller industries located in both rural and urban areas, managed by the sub-provincial level administration, mainly the commune and city administration were covered under collective ownership.

Industrial reform began on a modest scale. The measures were few and implemented in selected enterprises. Under central planning, industrial units were allotted a production quota, known as planned quota, which they were obliged to produce. The inputs and raw materials were supplied to the industrial units at state determined price. The units in turn, sold their output to the state, also at state determined price. The profits of the unit (equivalent to corporate income), if any, were remitted to the state. In case of loss, the state would subsidize. The prices of both input and output were divorced from cost of production and as a result, the profits and losses were largely notional. The reform began by allowing the industrial enterprises to produce beyond their output quota and sell the excess production in the market. Instead of diverting the entire profit to the state, the enterprises would pay a part of it as tax and use the balance to meet circulating and investment costs. They were allowed to arrange funds from the banks and to introduce bonus as an incentive to increase production and productivity.

Close on the heels came the policies and programmes to narrow down the state involvement in industries, allowing space to the private sector. In 1985, the state was spending one fourth of government revenue on subsidizing the losing enterprises. The alarming financial condition of most of the large industrial state owned enterprises forced the state to grant them autonomy and also agree to their privatization, though selectively. A series of measures were initiated to facilitate growth and development of the private sector, viewing it as a complement to the state sector. Barring the industries related to national security, industries engaged in the production of a few public goods and in hi-tech areas, the state began divesting its shares to a mix of state-private and in some cases, entirely to the private sector.

The industries under collective ownership, which were managed by the commune or city administration, were re-organized under Township and Village Enterprises. These included commune and brigade enterprises of central planning era and small industrial units managed by private individuals in reform period, then known as individual economy of the working people. Non-agricultural rural enterprises such as small factories and processing plants, mostly managed by different layers of local government, i.e., collective and town and township governments also came within its fold.

The reform of the industrial sector gained momentum in the 1990s, and particularly around 1995, with the worsening of the finances of not only the large state owned enterprises but also the small and medium units, which were responsible for about half of industrial output and employment each. Their performance declined so steadily over time that profits and taxes per unit of net capital stock declined from 24 per cent in 1978 to 12 percent in 1990 and further to 6 per cent in 1996. By the late 1990s, about half of these enterprises were in the red.

The reform at this time focused on transforming the ownership structure of the state owned enterprises into shareholding or joint stock companies, and wherever possible, their outright sale to private sector (a process known as disinvestment) while protecting the interests of the workers through a safety net of social security. In 1996, the state opened 1000 large state owned enterprises to privatization and joint stock companies and decided to relinquish the management of about 90 thousand small scale enterprises through merger, lease and sale. Most of these were overwhelmed with excess employment. For them reallocation of labour was the main concern. The restructuring of industries in the later half of the 1990s witnessed a massive lay-off of workers in state owned enterprises and urban collective enterprises. Mainly as a consequence, employment during the period 1996-2000 declined by 31 million in state owned units and another 15 million in urban collective owned units.

Privatization and outright closure of state owned enterprises reduced the financial burden of the state. State subsidy to losing enterprises already declined from 25.3 per cent of total government revenue in 1985 to 15.9 percent during the period 1986-93. The reform initiated in the early 1990s reduced this further and it averaged 3.7 per cent during the period 1994-2000.

The source and destination of industrial investment (in fixed assets) given in Table 6.11 show that the destination switched from state owned enterprises to jointly owned, share holding and foreign funded enterprises. (Annexure-A.4 gives the annual estimates since 1981) The source of investment shifted from state budget to domestic loan and foreign investment. In 1981-84, about one quarter of investment in fixed assets came from state budget. It averaged 4.2 per cent in 1992-2000. The relaxation on restrictions on foreign investment in industry began from the mid-1980s. The early measures in this direction were not adequate to attract foreign investment and its flow was meager in the 1980s. In the 1990s, the list of encouraged, discouraged and prohibited sectors in the industrial policy was reviewed to effect wider private sector participation. Tax benefits and concessional interest rates were provided to foreign investors in the area of export-oriented hi-tech industries. These coupled with administrative measures were instrumental in raising foreign capital inflow. From 1990 to 1997, net private capital inflow increased from US $ 8.1 billion to US $ 42.7 billion and foreign direct investment from US $ 3.5 billion to US $ 43.7 billion. In the process, China accounted for 25.6 per cent of the aggregate foreign direct investment that flowed to the 107 low and middle-income member countries of the World Bank. In domestic economy, foreign investment averaged 10.1 per cent of total investment in 1993-98.

Table 6.11: Investment by Source and Destination

(Percentage)

I. By Source	*State Budget*	*Domestic Loan*	*Foreign Investment*	*Fundraising and others*	*Total*
1. 1981 to 1984	24.0	13.4	4.3	58.3	100.0
2. 1985 to 1987	14.4	21.6	4.3	59.7	100.0
3. 1988 to 1991	8.2	20.6	6.1	65.1	100.0
4. 1992 to 2000	4.2	20.4	8.6	66.8	100.0
II. By Destination	SOE	COE	IE	Other Types	Total
5. 1980 to 1992	66.3	13.6	20.1	0	100.0
6. 1993 to 2000	53.6	15.4	13.4	17.6	100.0

Legend: 1. SOE=State Owned Enterprises. 2. COE=Collective Owned Enterprises. 3. IE=Individual Enterprises. 4. Other Types include joint owned economic units, shareholding economic units, foreign funded economic units.

Note: These are investment in fixed assets. The shares are calculated at current prices.

Investment, output and retail sales of private sector expanded in the 1990s. Private sector investment increased from 33.8 per cent of gross fixed investment in 1990 to 47.5 per cent in 1997. In total industrial output, the share of private sector increased from less than 10 per cent in 1990 to 36.8 percent in 1999 while that of state-owned and state controlled enterprises declined from 77.6 percent in 1978 to 54.6 per cent in 1990 and then to 27 per cent in 1999.[10] The share of private sector in retail sales of consumer goods increased from 28.7 per cent in 1990 to 62.7 per cent in 1999.

Under central planning, services sector was regarded as unproductive and hence not treated as a priority sector. It was covered under state owned enterprises and consequently, engulfed by all its inefficiencies. Most of the personal care and repair services were understaffed, inefficient and operated under loss. These were initially transferred to the Township and Village Industries and ultimately to the private sector. The high growth of income and employment in the services sector in the initial period of reform can mostly be attributed to privatization and expansion of market besides pent-up demand. The annual growth of value added in wholesale and retail trade and catering services was 15.7 per cent for the period 1978 to 1985; it reduced to 4.6 per cent per year in 1985-90 and then stabilized at 7.5 per cent per year in the 1990s (1991-2000). Posts and telecommunication also contributed to the growth of services sector in the 1990s; its annual growth was 31.4 per cent in 1991-99. These summed up the value added growth in services sector to 13.5 per cent per year and 9.2 per cent per year in the 1980s and 1990s respectively.

As a result of privatization and closure of state owned enterprises, the employment in state sector declined by about 46 million between 1996 and 2000. But during this period, 61 million were employed in other sectors of which 6.5 million in private enterprises, 10 million in co-operative units, limited liability corporations and shareholding corporations and 4.3 million in self-employment.

At the end of the day, the efficacy of industrial reform would be judged by the growth of industrial sector and level of living of industrial workers. The value added in industries (state and private sector taken together) increased by 12.7 per cent per year during the period 1980 to 1999. This far exceeds the growth of industrial sector value added of low income and lower middle-income countries, which are 3.4 per cent per year and 4 per cent per year respectively during the same period. The reform in the 1990s raised the industrial growth to 14.1 per cent per year in 1990-99 from 11.1 per cent per year in 1980-90. The high industrial growth changed the structure of the economy. The share of agriculture in GDP declined by 10 per cent point between 1990 and 1999 while that of industry and services sector increased by 8 per cent point and 2 per cent point respectively. In 1999, half of the GDP originated from industrial sector while agriculture and services sector accounted for 17 per cent and 33 per cent respectively.

The average growth of real wages in state owned enterprises and urban collective owned enterprises, which determine the level of living of the industrial workers, are given in Table 6.12. These indicate the favourable impact of reform on real wages throughout the two-decade period 1980-2000 barring a brief four year span of 1986-1989. The higher rate of growth of real wages in 1998-2000 underline the consolidation of industrial reform that began in the mid-1990s.

Table 6.12: Growth Rate of Real Wages of Workers and Staff

(percent per year, compound)

Period	*State Owned Enterprises*	*Urban Collective Enterprises*	*Others*
1. 1978 to 1985	5.25	5.23	—
2. 1986 to 1989	1.03	-0.28	3.68
3. 1990 to 1997	5.19	3.55	5.05
4. 1998 to 2000	10.17	6.80	6.73
5. 1978 to 1989	3.84	3.39	—
6. 1990 to 2000	6.55	4.44	5.51

VI
Fiscal Policy

Under central planning, the rates of taxation were fixed by the central government. The local (provincial and sub-provincial) governments used to collect revenue (excepting import revenue) and deposited with the central government. The central government, in turn, shared the revenue proceeds with the provinces using a revenue sharing formula.

The reform of the fiscal system began in the 1980s by setting out the center-province fiscal equation through a "fiscal contract system" under which the central government signed separate contract with each provincial government about sharing of revenue. The allocation of central subsidy to the provinces also came under the purview of this contract.

The yield of revenue and requirement of the provincial governments and the ten cities enjoying independent planning status differed so widely that a single allocation criteria was not found feasible. About half a dozen methods were evolved, earmarking a particular method for a province or group of provinces. The fiscal contract system was in force from 1980 to 1993, but often changed, with major changes occurring twice, in 1985 and 1988.

Along with the distribution mechanism, the taxation system came under reform. A set of direct and indirect taxation was introduced. In direct taxes, the rates of personal and corporate income taxation were made progressive. The existing indirect taxes were made broad based. The local administration was empowered to levy a few taxes based on the revenue need and taxable capacity of the area.

On 1st January 1994, a major tax and fiscal policy reform was initiated. In taxation, the authority of the national and the provincial governments was defined and the tax structure was rationalized. The taxes were grouped into three categories as central-fixed taxes, local-fixed taxes and shared taxes. The revenue from central-fixed taxes remained exclusively with the central government. Customs duties is a major revenue earning central-fixed tax. The local-fixed taxes are collected by the Local Tax Services of the provincial administration. The revenue from these taxes remained exclusively with the local governments. These include business tax, income tax of locally owned state enterprises and personal income tax. The shared taxes, as the name connotes, are shared with the provincial and local administration. The main shared taxes are value added tax, securities trading tax and natural resources tax. In order to administer these taxes, separate tax collection agencies were established at the national and regional levels, each being responsible for their tax collection. The central government constituted its own tax collection agency, namely the National Tax Service, to collect central-fixed taxes and shared taxes. The sharing of revenue in the manner described above dispensed with the fiscal contract system.

The tax structure was rationalized. Though there were more than twenty types of taxes in the country, four of them, viz., value added tax, operations tax, enterprise income tax and individual income tax together accounted for two third of the revenue. The value added tax was made broad-based, covering almost all the commodities and services. It became the major indirect tax shared by the national and local governments (75:25 ratio). A business tax was imposed on services, which were not covered by the value added tax. The enterprise tax was made uniform for all kinds of enterprises. This introduced transparency in the incidence of taxation and in revenue sharing.

The share of central and provincial governments in revenue and expenditure given in Table 6.13 underline the overwhelming impact of fiscal reform. The kink in revenue share of the central government in 1994 speaks for the tax reforms initiated then. The expenditure share of the central government underlines the sharpening of expenditure reform in the 1990s in which the state

Table 6.13: Central and Provincial Government Share in Revenue and Expenditure

(Percentage)

Period	*Revenue Central*	*Revenue Provinces*	*Period*	*Expenditure Central*	*Expenditure Provinces*
1. 1978	15.5	84.5	1. 1978	47.4	52.6
2. 1979 to 1982	23.4	76.6	2. 1979 to 1984	52.7	47.3
3. 1983 to 1990	34.9	65.1	3. 1985 to 1990	35.1	64.9
4. 1991 to 1993	26.2	73.8	4. 1991 to 2000	30.5	69.5
5. 1994 to 2000	51.1	48.9	5. 1978 to 2000	33.0	67.0

distanced itself from investing in economic sectors, allowing space to private sector. Privatization of state enterprises reduced government expenditure by way of reduction in state subsidy on losing enterprises. The state also reduced much of its spending on capital construction. The state investment was increasingly being earmarked for public goods and services, and in social sector, that is on education, health and welfare. The prevailing social security system, under which old, ill and disabled citizens are provided material assistance was also placed under reform. The pension scheme in the rural areas was tailored to the capacity of the local government in order to free it from the central government subsidy.

The state expenditure was contained by statutory prohibition of deficit financing through printing money. The borrowing restrictions on the local governments were more severe. The local governments at all levels were required to have their budgets balanced and were subjected to auditing their income and expenditure. The pattern of income and expenditure changed in the reform period. This altered the nature of the state budget. The budget was treated more as an instrument of macroeconomic management than balancing income and expenditure.

The state softened its stance in the matter of allocation of resources, facilitating the move from planned economy to market economy in which market forces determined the allocation of a greater part of the resources.

VII
Monetary Policy

The reform of the monetary system, like the fiscal reform, gathered momentum in the early 1990s. In central plan era, the People's Bank of China functioned as the central bank of the country and was charged with the responsibility of framing monetary policy, besides issuing currency. But, the control exercised by the Finance Ministry on money supply, credit and financial services was so overwhelming that the central bank became a "subsidiary" to the Finance Ministry.

In a major thrust, the Central Bank Law was promulgated in 1995. It did not allow complete freedom to the central bank but made it autonomous and answerable only to the state council, which is the highest organ of the state administration and can be equated with the cabinet in the western democracies.[11] The central bank had the sole responsibility of issuing currency and controlling money supply and was charged with the formulation and implementation of monetary policies. It served as government treasury, clearing center for financial transactions, holder of enterprise deposits and national savings bank. The central bank was involved in the conduct of macro-economic management and in the monitoring of the economic activities of the nation. For allocation of foreign exchange and for carrying out financial transactions with foreign firms and individuals, a separate institution, Bank of China was created.

The central bank, through the provisions of Budget Law enacted in 1995 was able to impose an element of financial discipline on the central government. Through its provisions, the central government was restricted from borrowing to finance current account deficit. The central government was allowed deficit financing in its capital account only; even this deficit required to be financed through government bonds. The central bank could resort to sale of bonds to finance the uncovered gap between the income and expenditure of the government. The central bank could impose financial restrictions on the local governments by way of controlling their bond issuance and restricting borrowing in the financial market. These in effect, gave the central bank the mandate for formulating monetary policy independent of the local governments, marking a shift in the center-province financial equation from central plan era when the local governments were empowered to borrow independently. The local government's influence on monetary policy and credit allocation decisions waned.

Besides the People's Bank of China, which is the central bank and the Bank of China, which deals with foreign exchange transactions, the banking system included a number of specialized banks such as, Agricultural Bank of China, China Investment Bank, Industrial and Commercial Bank of China, Import-Export Bank, People's Construction Bank of China, Bank of Communications, People's Insurance Company of China, and a chain of rural and urban credit cooperatives. The specialized banks catered to the needs of specific sectors. These were transformed into commercial banks and made responsible for their financial performance. Non-bank institutions were created as a part of the financial sector reform. The stock market, as a part of the financial sector reform, expanded rapidly in the 1990s. The stock market capitalization increased from a mere US$2 billion in 1990 to US$331 billion in 1999. The number of listed companies increased from only fourteen in 1990 to 950 in 1999.

The management of the exchange rate was placed under the central bank. The exchange rate was determined in the market under the watchful eyes of the central bank, which remained responsible for maintaining its stability. The central bank participated in the foreign exchange market to buy and sell foreign currencies to keep the exchange rate of Yuan stable.

Until the 31st December 1993, there existed a two tier exchange rate, viz., the official rate and the market rate. The latter was also known as swap rate in China. From January 1, 1994 these two rates were unified. The unified rate as a general rule became higher than the official rate but lower than the market or swap rate. This raised the cost of foreign exchange for those who used to receive it at official rate (that is at a rate lower than the unified rate). The state provided them subsidy for a period of three years to enable them to acquire the same amount of foreign exchange. Then, in December 1996, the currency was made convertible in current account, and thereby listed China in the IMFs Article VIII member country. It did not, and rightly so, move to capital account convertibility.

The transition from central planning to a market based economy ensured the macro-economic balance with a moderate level of price inflation mainly due to prudent monetary policy.[12] Even this moderate inflation cannot entirely be attributed to reform policies as there are considerable differences of opinion among theoreticians about the causes of price inflation during this period. The Chinese economy is integrated with the rest of the world with a reduced import tariff rate (less than 20 per cent) and removal of most of the quantitative restrictions on import. Most of the exchange control on trade and trade related transactions are also abolished. The foreign assets of the central bank increased. The foreign exchange reserve increased from US $ 34.5 billion in 1990 to US $ 157.7 billion in 1999. The foreign debt remained at a manageable level, at 15 per cent of the Gross National Product in 1998, which only seven of the 103 member countries of the World Bank could manage.

VIII
Price Policy

Price in a centrally planned economy does not reflect the real cost as it is set by the state instead of being determined in the market through the interaction between demand and supply. As a result, same commodity is priced differently at different sources and also at destinations. Price reform by way of allowing it to be set by the interaction between demand and supply in the market and in the absence of a market, raising by the state to reflect its real cost, was an integral part of the transition to a market economy. It began with the introduction of a dual price mechanism, in which the prices of a few goods were administered by the state while that of others were determined in the market. There were also dual price of the same good. In other words, a commodity could face both state determined price and market price. The market price as a rule is higher than the official price. As a result of the price subsidy offered by the state to the consumers the co-existence of official price and market price could promote market economy without effecting welfare losses to those benefited by the official price.

The price reform began with agriculture. Farm prices were increased by 22 per cent in 1979. In stages, the state allowed the prices of non-agricultural products, such as consumer goods, to float in the market. By mid-1990s, prices of most of the goods and services were freed from state control and were determined in the market. The price control (that is dual pricing) remains for items that are critical for the national economy. For example, the prices of key raw materials such as coal, steel, electricity, and service items such as, rail transport are still administered by the state, but reviewed periodically in an effort to reflect its real cost.

Price began to play a greater role in setting the course of production and distribution of a large number of commodities. The state through a kind of administered price mechanism still bears some price subsidy though its quantum declined with price reform. In the 1980s, annual price subsidy ranged from 12 to 14 per cent of total expenditure of the central and local governments; it came down to 5 to 7 per cent in 1993-2000. The average price subsidy for the period 1993-2000 was 6 per cent of total expenditure of central and local governments as against 13 per cent in 1981-90. About three-fourth of the price subsidy is earmarked for grain, cotton and edible oil. The essentiality of price subsidy can be judged from the case of grain which arises from the difference between its procurement price and sale price. The state has to raise the procurement price of grain due to increase in its cost of production. If the procurement price is not kept in line with the cost of production, the farmers will not find grain production remunerative. This is a risk, which no country, particularly China can take as it may lead to decline in grain production and, consequently increase its food dependency on other countries. The state also cannot raise the sale price of grain beyond a point as it will raise the cost of living of those who are net buyers of grain. The poorest in rural areas such as the agricultural workers being net buyers of grain are likely to be the worst affected in such a situation. It would generate a kind of resentment and turmoil in the society, causing hardship not only to the poorer agricultural workers but also the urbanites, so that the state does not have an alternative to continue with the subsidy. The talk of an accurate price in agriculture, particularly in case of grain does not make sense in a low-income developing country where the diet of the majority of the population is composed of grain, and a large section of the people in lower income group are net buyers of food. Since the state cannot deny the responsibility of providing food, there is no alternative to price subsidy until such time the people in general and particularly the poor, acquire the purchasing power to buy food at the prices prevailing in the market.

IX
Regional Planning

Under central planning, the regional development strategy was framed by the central government and implemented by the provincial governments. The growth trajectory of the provinces, particularly of the less well endowed ones were set by the transfer of resources from the central government, canalized through the state budget.

The reforms initiated a process of decentralization of power from central to provincial governments and also from provincial to local governments. The provinces and the local administration were allowed greater autonomy in managing their economic affairs and space in charting their growth path in the environs of comparative advantage. The development of the provinces thus became more associated with their own policy initiatives, rather than the policies of the central government.

In order to exploit the growth potentials to the maximum, regionally differentiated policies were applied in the initial years of reform. The coastal areas were more developed and endowed with essential infrastructure such as transportation and communication facilities, availability of managerial expertise and skilled labour. The foreign investments, both institutional and direct, were canalized to the coastal areas by a series of promotional measures such as, concession in tax and interest on capital, project allocation, foreign exchange, trade and even on revenue sharing with the central government. Until the late 1990s, 10 inland provinces received only 20 per cent of the foreign capital inflow. The direction of investment to the developed areas by state action *prima facie* appears as retrograde policies. The reason behind directing foreign investment to developed areas, to begin with, may lie in the premise that unless it is effective in these areas, how can they be expected to succeed in the poor and backward areas with weak or non-existent infrastructure. The initial flow of foreign investment was directed to four Special Economic Zones created in the coastal region. With their success, 14 coastal cities were opened to foreign investment. A pragmatic decision, indeed. Subsequently, foreign investment was allowed in inland and border areas and promotional measures granted to the Special Economic Zones and coastal cities were also extended there. Some reform measures, such as those relating to foreign investment benefited the developed areas more than others. In tandem, there are reform policies, which benefited the backward areas more than the developed areas. For example, being a net exporter of primary products, the price reform resulting in the rise in raw materials and energy prices, benefited the inland and backward provinces more than others.

The state, in the central plan era, was directly engaged in international trade. It began de-regulation of trade policy in order to allow trading with the rest of the world under global economic trends and compulsions. The private sector entered into trading activities. The provincial and local governments and some of the enterprises were permitted to trade directly with other nations.

There was concentration of trade in the developed areas. The trade-GDP ratio of the coastal region was about five times as compared to the rest of the country. A three-year average (1998-2000) of the provincial shares of export, import and total trade given in Table 6.14 marks the newly acquired importance of Guangdong on the canvas of regional inequality. Guangdong alone accounts for about two-fifth of the nation's trade. Shanghai and Jiangsu together account for another one-fifth. These three provinces together generate nearly 60 per cent of nation's export and import. In contrast, one-tenth of the total trade is originated in 22 provinces, which account for more than two-third of the population. The share of trade in the provinces is also not related to the income shares.

Table 6.14: Share of Export and Import: Average for 1998-2000

(Percentage)

Provinces	*Export*	*Import*	*Total*
1. Guangdong	39.6	38.0	38.9
2. Shanghai	9.3	12.3	10.7
3. Jiangsu	9.7	9.3	9.5
A. Total: 1 to 3	58.6	59.6	59.1
4. Beijing	3.3	7.2	5.0
5. Tianjin	3.1	4.2	3.6
6. Liaoning	4.2	4.2	4.2
7. Zhejiang	7.3	4.3	5.9
8. Fujian	5.6	4.6	5.1
9. Shandong	6.3	5.4	5.9
B. Total: 4 to 9	29.8	29.9	29.7
C. Total: Nine Provinces (A) + (B)	88.4	89.5	88.8
D. Remaining 22 Provinces	11.6	10.5	11.2

The revenue generation in the provinces is observed to be unequal. Five provinces, viz., Beijing, Shanghai, Jiangsu, Zhejiang and Guangdong is the home of 18.8 per cent of the population whereas they generate 39.5 per cent of total revenue and 47 percent of the four major taxes, viz., value added tax, operations tax, enterprise income tax and individual income tax in 2000. Adding Liaoning and Shandong to these five, seven provinces account for less than 30 per cent of the population but 51.5 of total revenue and 58.2 per cent of revenue from four major taxes. The share of revenue in these provinces matches with their income share.

The GDP growth rates of the provinces are given in Table 6.15. For the period 1978-95, treating annual growth rate of 10 per cent and above as "high" and less than 10 per cent as "low growth rate", thirteen provinces are classified in "high growth rate" and seventeen provinces in "low growth rate" category. The growth rate in all but one (Hebei) of these thirteen high growth provinces in 1996-2000 are lower than in 1978-95. In the low growth category, the seventeen provinces are almost equally divided; in nine provinces, the growth rate in 1996-2000 are more than in 1978-95 while it is just the opposite in eight provinces where the growth rate in 1996-2000 are less than in 1978-95. Characteristically, the growth, particularly after mid-1990s have wider regional spread.

The regional spread (disparity) of a variable can be measured by (a) the range of values from the maximum to the minimum among the provinces and (b) a composite index of the measure of dispersion, known as coefficient of variation, which is the standard deviation of the variable expressed as percentage of its mean or average value. The coefficient of variation is known for its comparability between variables when their average values differ. The inter-provincial disparity of GDP growth rates measured by these indicators given in Table 6.16 show that the regional disparity in growth rates in 1996-2000 is almost half of that witnessed until the mid-1990s. The reduced regional disparity in the growth rates in 1996-2000 is caused by two factors. These are : (a) The high growth provinces until the mid-1990s witnessed reduction in the growth rate in 1996-2000. (b) In an opposing situation, the low growth provinces until the mid-1990s witnessed increase in the growth rate in 1996-2000.

Table 6.15: GDP Growth Rates in Provinces

(percent per year, compound)

	Province	*1978-95*	*1996-2000*	*1978-2000*
1.	Beijing	9.8	10.2	9.9
2.	Tianjin	8.9	10.6	9.2
3.	Hebei	10.2	10.5	10.2
4.	Shanxi	8.8	8.1	8.7
5.	Inner Mongolia	13.0	9.2	12.3
6.	Liaoning	8.8	8.6	8.8
7.	Jilin	9.5	8.9	9.4
8.	Heilongjiang	4.8	8.5	5.5
9.	Shanghai	9.1	11.0	9.5
10.	Jiangsu	12.8	10.9	12.4
11.	Zhejiang	13.8	10.6	13.2
12.	Anhui	10.7	9.4	10.5
13.	Fujian	13.7	11.4	13.3
14.	Jiangxi	10.4	8.9	10.2
15.	Shandong	11.9	10.7	11.7
16.	Henan	10.9	9.1	10.6
17.	Hubei	10.5	10.2	10.4
18.	Hunan	8.7	9.3	8.8
19.	Guangdong	14.2	10.3	13.5
20.	Guangxi	7.9	8.0	7.9
21.	Hainan	12.3	8.0	11.5
22.	Sichuan	9.5	8.5	9.3
23.	Guizhou	9.1	8.6	9.0
24.	Yunnan	9.9	7.9	9.5
25.	Tibet	8.3	10.1	8.6
26.	Shaanxi	9.1	8.9	9.1
27.	Gansu	8.6	8.7	8.6
28.	Qinghai	6.8	8.8	7.2
29.	Nignxia	8.9	8.7	8.9
30.	Xinjiang	11.1	8.4	10.6
31.	China	9.9	8.3	9.6

Table 6.16: Regional Variation in GDP Growth Rates

Indicator	*1978-95*	*1996-2000*	*1978-2000*
1. Range	9.4	3.5	8.0
2. Standard Deviation	2.08	1.02	1.82
3. Coefficient of Variation (%)	20.6	10.9	18.3

The inter-provincial variation of income and expenditure levels is given in Table 6.17. The inter-provincial disparity of per capita GDP is greater than per capita living expenditure, which in turn, is greater than per capita food expenditure, a trend reminiscent of central plan era. The inter-provincial variation in per capita net income in rural areas increased until the mid-1990s, but showed signs of abatement thereafter. Much of this disparity is eliminated if three developed urbanized areas of the country, viz., Beijing, Tianjin and Shanghai are excluded. For example, in 2000, the ratio of maximum to minimum per capita GDP among the 31 provinces is 13 times; it reduces to 5.1 times when calculated excluding these three provinces. In the central plan era, high regional disparity was accompanied by low average income. In the reform period, a smaller or similar disparity is centered on a higher average income.

Table 6.17: Inter-Provincial Variation in Income and Expenditure

Indicator/Year	*All Provinces*	*All Provinces*	*Excluding Three Provinces★*	*Excluding Three Provinces★*
	Maximum/ Minimum	*Coefficient of Variation (%)*	*Maximum/ Minimum*	*Coefficient of Variation (%)*
1. Per Capita Net Income In Rural Areas				
a) 1985	3.2	31.1	2.1	18.3
b) 1990	4.4	40.1	2.6	24.4
c) 1995	4.8	46.3	3.4	35.1
d) 2000	4.2	43.4	3.2	33.7
2. Per Capita GDP in 2000	13.0	75.9	5.1	43.2
3. Per Capita LE in 2000	3.8	41.9	3.0	31.7
4. Per Capita FE in 2000	3.5	34.1	2.7	27.4
5. Average Wages of Workers and Staff in 2000	2.9	30.6	2.4	23.9

★ The three provinces excluded are Beijing, Tianjin and Shanghai.

Legend GDP = Gross Domestic Product; LE = Living Expenditure; FE = Food Expenditure.

Note: The number of provinces are 29 in 1985 and 1990, 30 in 1995 and 31 in 2000.

Inter-provincial disparity in the consumption of wage goods is low. The inter-provincial disparity measured by coefficient of variation is 25 per cent in case of edible oil and 13 per cent in grain consumption. In case of meat items, the coefficient of variation is high for individual items of fish, egg and meat consumption. The disparity becomes low when the consumption of all these items are taken together. This indicates the localized pattern of consumption of items of animal protein.

The urban-rural differential in per capita consumption was less than 3.0 until 1980. It reduced to 2.5 during the period 1981 to 1987. Thereafter it increased and remained in the range of 3.0 to 3.5 during the period 1990 to 1999. These calculations are made without correcting for urban-rural price differential.[13] The urban-rural differential in per capita consumption is manifested in the consumption shares of rural and urban population. The consumption share of rural population declined from about two-third of the total consumption in the early 1980s to 45.2 per cent in 2000. The share of rural population reduced as a result of urbanization. But fall in rural consumption share is sharper.[14]

The regional inequality in income and consumption is reflected on the poverty scene. Chen and Wang have presented the rural poverty ratio (number of poor as percentage of total population) for 31 provinces in 1996 derived from the official poverty line. The national average of rural poverty ratio in 1996 is 14.52 per cent; it ranges from less than one percent in Shanghai and Guangdong to 52.76 per cent in Tibet.[15] The impact of living expenditure on rural poverty is not uniform across provinces despite negative association between the two. The correlation coefficient between poverty ratio and average living expenditure is –0.73. The inter-regional variation in poverty ratio is twice of that of living expenditure. There are nine provinces with poverty ratio less than 5 per cent. Recognizing that 5 per cent of the people in a society may constitute disabled and handicapped and that they cannot be covered by developmental programmes, 22 provinces can said to be afflicted with poverty. The inter-provincial variation in both poverty ratio and per capita living expenditure among these 22 provinces becomes low, but the variation in poverty ratio turns out to be three times of that of average expenditure.[16] The wider variation in poverty ratio relative to expenditure underlines the structural reasons for poverty.

X
Reform Programmes of World Bank and IMF

Throughout the 1950s and 1960s, the World Bank theorem was that high growth rate can solve the problem of poverty and unemployment of the developing countries. The developing countries on their own cannot raise the rate of economic growth as they lack investment. The developed countries of the capitalist world agreed to finance part of the investment by way of loan and aid. The income growth achieved as a result of this investment was believed to percolate from the top (rich) to the bottom (poor) sections of the population. The income of the poor would increase; unemployment and poverty would reduce.

By the late 1960s, when it was realized that the developing countries were nowhere near solving their problems of unemployment and poverty, the World Bank commissioned David Morawetz to trace the pattern of income growth in developing countries in 1950-75. It reported: the developing countries have not experienced the desired growth in income and whatever little growth has come about, has not been shared equally between nations or between its population.[17] The mandarins of 1818 H Street in Washington D.C. pinned the sonic of the blame on inefficiency and mismanagement in developing countries but in course of time realized that equity in the distribution of the fruits of growth is as important as the rate of growth and in the matter of raising the levels of welfare and in improving the quality of life of the people, composition of growth may be as important as the growth itself.

Thus originated the idea that the maladies of unemployment and poverty of the developing world cannot be removed relying solely on income growth. The theorem was changed to increase in income of the poor directly that is, bypassing the general growth process. This witnessed the formulation two types of income re-distributive poverty alleviation programmes in the early 1970s. These are: (a) asset generation programme and (b) employment generation programme. The asset generation programmes are designed for those poor having the requisite skill so that state assistance combined with private entrepreneurship and skill produces a regular flow of income which, when added to the income originating from the general growth process, allows them to cross the poverty line. The employment generation programmes are generally offered to those poor who have nothing but their raw labour power to sell. The latter programmes do not allow them to cross the poverty line permanently. In the absence of employment provided by such programmes, they may rejoin the poor group. Almost all the developing countries since then are implementing these programmes as a part of the poverty alleviation strategy.

Initially, the International Monetary Fund (IMF) was not so much vocal about the strategy of economic development that its member countries would pursue. By the early 1980s, the financial position of not only the less developed countries but also of many middle-income countries became precarious for a variety of reasons. The IMF which was observing the activities of its sister organization across the road, entered the scene as the custodian of international monetary system. Charged with the responsibility of promoting international monetary co-operation, facilitating the expansion and balanced growth of international trade and to promote exchange rate stability, the International Monetary Fund formulated its own package of economic reform and liberalization, which is currently underway in the developing countries world wide. Briefly, the programme contains:

(a) short-term stabilization policies in order to correct the balance of payments disequilibria through adjustment in the exchange rate, ensuring macro-economic balances through curtailment of government expenditure, monetary liquidity and market liberalization through elimination of subsidies and price controls; and
(b) long-term economic reforms under structural adjustment programmes covering de-regulation of industry, liberalization of trade, elimination of protective tariff barriers, privatization of state enterprises and financial institutions, streamlining of the state sector, privatization of social programmes and rationalization of the tax structure.

The Bretton Woods' reform programmes are thus more or less synonymous with relaxation, and even removal, of state control in economic activities, allowing a greater play for market. By and large, they focus on the economy-wide changes in the initial stages, with the sectoral issues being tackled later in a more gradual manner.

However, China's implementation of the reform programmes in both form and content has not followed the scheme as described above. China maintained its own coverage and speed in pursuing a particular programme. True, the reform in the 1980s was not all embracing. The equilibrating role of market was a concern for China though efficiency and economic growth remained high on the agenda. It's traditional concern about the social problems arising from market mechanism made them extremely careful in deregulating markets. There is indeed a trade-off between efficiency gains out of the functioning of the market and social problems, which has forced, not unjustifiably, them to pursue the reforms programmes in a step-by-step approach and careful in deregulating markets. In view of the vastness of the country and its varying levels of spatial development, they considered unwise to apply a uniform strategy throughout the country. In the 1980s, the reform was complete in agriculture and was in formative stage in other real and financial sectors. The real thrust came in the 1990s when it concentrated on (i) foreign exchange and external sector (ii) tax and fiscal areas (iii) financial sector (iv) state owned enterprises and (v) social safety net. This way, China's reform programmes are shaped and implemented entirely by themselves, though unlike the central planning days, considerable amount of interaction was maintained with the outside world.

XI
Why Planning ?

The implementation of the economic reform programmes (in a typical developing country) creates an environment in which (a) market predominates (b) private sector expands (c) state sector enterprises are made autonomous and exposed to market forces as private sector (d) trade with the rest of the world operates under global economic trends and compulsions. The state confines its activities to the creation of suitable environment for growth and development rather than directly taking part in production and trade.

As the economy is deregulated and decisions are based on market, the state cannot remain a silent spectator to the emerging vulnerabilities. The dismantling of state control and regulatory measures and putting in place a market based system makes it necessary to re-define the role of planning. The change in the planning process under economic reform takes place due to the change in the role of the state from a direct producer of goods and services to a facilitator. The state would be expected to provide infrastructure and social services, and to enter into the areas where private initiative is not forthcoming. In the developing countries, the state cannot altogether shed the responsibility of social welfare, particularly for the poor and the disadvantaged, and areas such as population control, environmental protection, health and education.

The market system has brought bountiful benefits since the days of Adam Smith. It has also created large scale disruption at every turn of history and wrecked havoc on the lives of millions of people. This warrants state intervention for the expansion of the market and to make it operate freely, competitively and with accessibility.

The strong point of the market is efficiency. Its weak point is that it has only a short-term view. The market prices are more influenced by available supply and demand in a limited time horizon. As such, the price mechanism is inadequate to protect factors (such as environment and ecology), which have long-term consequences. The market needs prospective information beyond those accompanying the price. This necessitates state intervention and planning. Some of the long-term costs can be built into current costs and prices, but that is also possible only through intervention. In whichever area the society has to take a long-term view, state intervention and planning becomes necessary. Planning in this context means taking a long-term view, setting goals and devising strategies to achieve these goals. There are complementarities between market as an efficiency-promoting device and planning as an instrument of establishing behavioural pattern appropriate for achieving the targets set out in the plan.

The reform process requires strong interventionist policy in almost all the areas of the economy. So long as there is a government, it has to do things. This ensures state interference. The issue boils down to the stage or the level at which the state should intervene. The implementation of the policies of economic reform does not mean that the state will abandon its role in the economy and planning; it would only re-focus it suitably to make it more effective. The role of planning under the economic reform is to devise the best and the most productive strategy applying the least but the most effective interventions and not relying only on efficiency and growth.

XII
Comparing China

How does Chinese economy compare with the low and lower middle-income countries in the world, and with India in particular? The comparison is made in Table 6.18. In 1999, with a little over one-fifth of world population, China accounts for only 3.4 per cent of world GNP, when it is measured conventionally, that is using the prevailing exchange rate of US dollar to Chinese Yuan. Its share rises to 10.6 per cent if GNP is measured using Purchasing Power Parity (PPP) exchange rate.[18] As it has recently been graduated from low income to lower middle income group, its per capita GNP is 16.7 per cent lower than the average of LMI countries when GNP is measured in terms of PPP and 35 per cent less than conventionally measured GNP.

Table 6.18: Share of Economies in 1999

Indicator	*LI*	*LMI*	*UMI*	*India*	*China*
1. Number of countries	53	35	19	1	1
2. Population (%)	40.5	35.0	9.6	16.7	20.9
3. GNP – Conventional (%)	3.4	8.6	9.6	1.5	3.4
4. GNP – PPP (%)	11.1	21.4	12.2	5.5	10.6
5. Per Capita GNP: Conventional with China =100	53	154	628	58	100
6. Per Capita GNP: PPP with China =100	54	120	253	65	100

A comparison between India and China on contentious issues is interesting on more counts than one. The two countries are neighbours with a long boundary. Both began the pursuit of development almost at the same time; China in October 1949 when it proclaimed the People's Republic and India in August 1947 when it gained freedom from nearly two centuries of colonial rule. Both took some time to extend its rule to the entire area. India had to consolidate the Princely Estates. China took time to get rid of the "enemies" of revolution throughout the country. Their similarity lies in low level of development with a population, huge compared to the resources. Their initial development strategy differed as China adopted central planning whereas India practiced mixed economy. With economic reforms, China aligned itself with mixed economy. These apart, the sharp difference in the political governance of the two countries makes the comparison meaningful, and interesting as well.

The management of Indian agriculture and the agricultural operations in China in the post-central plan era typify joint state-private sector phenomenon. In India, the state provides the extension facilities and makes large scale investment, for example in mega-irrigation projects, which can not be financed by individual farm households. The acreage and type of crop is decided by millions of farmers in the countryside. The state does not interfere in this decision making process except through some price and fiscal signals. The Responsibility System in China's agriculture operationally is not very different from the Indian system.

The operations of the industrial sector of the two countries are also comparable. China's industrial policies in the reform period resembles to India's two initial Industrial Policy Resolutions (IPR), in 1948 and in 1956. IPR 1948 had a dominant state sector, which did not facilitate industrial growth. So came IPR 1956 with relaxation of state control and allowing the private sector to engage and expand in several areas of industry. The regulation of state owned industries in China in the reform period characterize a similar situation. The collective owned industries in China are close comparisons of the industries in small scale and tiny sector in India, which are managed by private individuals or co-operatives. As a part of the economic reform measures, the industrial policy adopted by

India in 1991 bear close resemblance with the industrial policies in China in the 1990s.

A system of administered prices covering items of both intermediate use and final consumption, most of which are wage goods, has long been the feature of Indian planning. This creates mostly dual, sometimes multiple pricing of a product. This dual price mechanism through the administered prices has been viewed as a means to ensure equity and social justice in Indian planning despite its potentially adverse impact on the efficiency and growth. The reform in China introduced a dual price mechanism similar to that existed in India. However, India has considerably withdrawn the administered price mechanism since it began its reform programme in 1991. The price reform in China is basically along this course.

The state subsidy on grain is a contentious issue in both India and China. It has been with China since the beginning of the People's Republic. India entered into a regime of food subsidy over a period of time. There are criticisms on price subsidy on grain in both these countries, arising from an identical fashion. Food subsidy is essential for both. India and China, each with billion-plus population and mouths to feed, and for a vast majority of them without the adequate purchasing power, the opportunity cost of withdrawal of food subsidy may be enormous. It can, at the most be targeted to specific groups.

REFERENCES

1. The Constitution originally promulgated by the People's Republic and adopted by the National People's Congress in 1954 was changed twice before, in 1975 and 1978.
2. Lardy, Nicholas R. *Integrating China into the Global Economy*, Brookings Institution Press, 2003, Chapter-1.
3. The World Bank in 1999 classified (a) 53 countries with per capita GNP less than US $ 755 in low-income group, (b) 35 countries with per capita GNP ranging from US $ 756 to US $ 2995 in lower middle-income group (c) 19 countries with per capita GNP ranging from US $ 2996 to US $ 9265 in upper middle income group. China, with per capita GNP of US $ 780 in 1999 is classified in lower middle-income group.
4. The official tabulations from household survey data suggest rising income

inequality in post-reform rural China. However, it has been argued that the structural changes in China's rural economy have not been properly reflected in the methods used to process raw survey data, and hence this outcome. Using micro data for four provinces, Ravallion and Chen find that two-thirds of the conventionally measured increase in inequality in 1985-90 vanishes when market-based valuation methods are used and allowances are made for regional cost of living differences. Martin Ravallion and Shaohua Chen, *When Economic Reform is Faster than Statistical Reform: Measuring and Explaining Inequality in Rural China*, World Bank, March 1998, also in *Oxford Bulletin of Economics and Statistics*, Vol. 61, pp. 33-56, 1999.

5. The consumption and income distributions are available at the prices prevailing in the year of survey and not at constant or comparable prices. The rural income distributions for the years 1990, 1995 and 2000 have been converted into 1985 prices using the General Consumer Price Index for rural areas. Fractile specific price differentials that might exist in such data are not eliminated.
6. The distribution corrected growth rate of private consumption is calculated as 1 minus the Gini Index multiplied by the annual rate of growth of private consumption. Gini Index measures the extent to which the distribution of consumption among individuals (or households, as the case may be) within a country/region deviates from a perfectly equal distribution. The growth rates of distribution corrected private consumption would be lower than the growth rate of nominal consumption depending on the nature of consumption distribution. Among the 87 countries (for which the growth rates have been computed), the distribution corrected growth rates are lower by 50 to 70 per cent of the actual growth rates in 57 countries. Table 2, p 276, *Attacking Poverty, World Development Report, 2000-2001,* Oxford University Press, 2000.
7. Martin Ravallion and Shaohua Chen, "What Can New Survey Data Tell Us about Recent Changes in Distribution and Poverty?", *World Bank Economic Review* Vol.11, No. 2, pp. 357-382, quoted in World Development Report 2000-2001, The World Bank.
8. The estimate of poverty reduction is based on the poverty ratio of about 30 percent in 1978 and 3 percent in 2000.
9. The data relate to 53 low income and 35 lower middle income countries. Among these 88 countries the annual growth rate of 44 countries range from one to three per cent. Table 8, p. 289, *Attacking Poverty, World Development Report, 2000-2001,* Oxford University Press, 2000.
10. State-owned means cent per cent state ownership. State-controlled means the state has 51 per cent or more shares in joint ventures or joint stock companies. Collectives refer to urban collective enterprises and rural township-village enterprises. The remaining, including foreign firms are private enterprises.
11. In the context of the Central Bank – Finance Ministry tussle for authority, I. G. Patel, Governor of India's central bank, the Reserve Bank of India, in the late 1970s and early 1980s points out two factors that go against complete freedom of a central bank in monetary matters. First, it is not easy to define in operational terms what the monetary matters are. Second, economic policy is about dealing with events as they unfold so that one cannot always be sure what should be done, when, and in what amount. I. G. Patel, *Glimpses of India's Economic Policy: An Insider's View*, Oxford University Press, 2002, p. 186.

12. The price rise measured by the General Retail Price Index averaged 5.9 per cent per year in 1978-2000. During these 23 year period, rise in the General Retail Price Index was excessive in five years; it rose by 18.5 per cent in 1988, 17.8 per cent in 1989, 13.2 per cent in 1993, 21.7 per cent in 1994 and 14.8 per cent in 1995. Excluding these, the price rise in the remaining 18 years of reform period averaged to 2.8 per cent per year.
13. The price inflation in urban areas is more than in rural areas excepting 1989-90. The annual average inflation rate measured by General Consumer Price Index in rural and urban areas are 9.4 per cent and 12.1 per cent respectively in 1985-88, 11.9 per cent and 8.8 per cent respectively in 1989-90 and 6.9 per cent and 8.2 per cent respectively in 1991-2000.
14. The consumption share of rural areas averaged 63.5 per cent in 1978 to 1985, 56.7 per cent in 1986 to 1992 and 48.2 per cent in 1993 to 2000. In 1982, rural areas contained 79.1 per cent of population and 63.7 per cent of consumption, implying a consumption-population ratio of 0.81. This came down to 0.71 in 2000 with 63.8 per cent of population and 45.2 per cent of consumption.
15. Shaohua Chen and Yan Wang, "China's Growth and Poverty Reduction: Recent Trends Bewteen 1990 and 1999", Table A6, pp. 218-19, in *Impact of the East Asian Financial Crisis Revisited*, (ed) Shahid Khandker, The World Bank Institute and Philippine Institute for Development Studies, 2002.
16. The inter-provincial variation measured by coefficient of variation is (a) 39.5 per cent for per capita living expenditure and 82.3 per cent for poverty ratio, among 31 provinces (b) 18.0 per cent for per capita living expenditure and 54.2 per cent for poverty ratio, among the 22 provinces where poverty ratio exceeds 5 per cent.
17. D. Morawetz, *Twenty Five Years of Economic Development 1950-75*, John Hopkins Press, Baltimore, 1977.
18. Purchasing Power Parity (PPP) is an exchange rate at which a fixed basket of goods of a country would be available in another country. If a basket of goods is available in China at 100 Chinese Yuan and the same basket of goods can be procured in the USA at US $ 20, then the exchange rate is US $ 20 to 100 Chinese Yuan, or in other words, one US dollar to five Chinese Yuan. PPP exchange rate depends critically on the composition of the basket. The exchange rate based on PPP can compare the standard of living between the countries more efficiently than the conventional exchange rates. It is because, if the value of Chinese Yuan falls compared to the US dollar, the GNP of China measured in US dollar will reduce by the same proportion. But, this decline in the dollar value of China's GNP does not make the Chinese worse off. The level of living of the Chinese will not alter if the real income measured in Chinese Yuan remains unchanged. Thus, income based on PPP exchange rates allows inter-country comparison of the standard of living more accurately than the income estimates based on conventional exchange rate. The rankings of countries by GNP do not alter significantly in these two measures. The World Bank has estimated the GNP of 207 small and large countries of varying levels of development using both conventional and PPP exchange rate. The ranks of 126 countries (countries with population exceeding one million) under these two methods are identical for 9 countries and in another 17 countries it differ by just one rank. For these 126 countries, the rank correlation coefficient between the two is estimated as 0.97.

Annexure A.1

Consumption and Investment Rates

Year	*Consumption Rate (%)*	*Investment Rate (%)*	*Household Consumption Rate (%)*	*Government Consumption Rate (%)*
1	*2*	*3*	*4*	*5*
1978	62.1	38.2	78.6	21.4
1979	64.3	36.2	76.6	23.4
1980	65.4	34.9	77.9	22.1
1981	67.5	32.3	78.7	21.3
1982	66.3	32.1	78.8	21.2
1983	66.2	33.0	79.2	20.8
1984	65.5	34.5	78.3	21.7
1985	65.7	38.5	79.5	20.5
1986	64.6	38.0	79.1	20.9
1987	63.2	36.7	80.0	20.0
1988	63.7	37.4	81.5	18.5
1989	64.1	37.0	80.7	19.3
1990	62.0	35.2	80.2	19.8
1991	61.8	35.3	78.5	21.5
1992	61.7	37.3	78.1	21.9
1993	58.5	43.5	77.7	22.3
1994	57.4	41.3	77.7	22.3
1995	57.5	40.8	80.1	19.9
1996	58.5	39.3	80.4	19.6
1997	58.2	38.0	80.0	20.0
1998	58.7	37.4	79.6	20.4
1999	60.1	37.1	79.1	20.9
2000	61.3	36.2	78.6	21.4

Note. Items in Cols. (2) and (3) are expressed as percentage to GDP at current prices. Items in Cols. (4) and (5) are expressed as percentage to total consumption at current prices.

Source: Table 3-12, pp. 61-62, China Statistical Yearbook 2001, National Bureau of Statistics of China, China Statistics Press, Bejing.

Annexure A.2

Gross Domestic Product and its Distribution

Year	*Primary*	*Secondary*	*Tertiary*	*Total GDP*	*Share (%) Primary*	*Share (%) Secondary*	*Share (%) Tertiary*
1	*2*	*3*	*4*	*5*	*6*	*7*	*8*
1978	100.0	100.0	100.0	100.0	28.1	48.2	23.7
1979	106.1	108.2	107.8	107.6	31.2	47.4	21.4
1980	104.6	122.9	114.2	116.0	30.1	48.5	21.4
1981	111.9	125.2	126.2	122.1	31.8	46.4	21.8
1982	124.8	132.1	142.6	133.1	33.3	45.0	21.7
1983	135.1	145.8	164.3	147.6	33.0	44.6	22.4
1984	152.6	166.9	196.1	170.0	32.0	43.3	24.7
1985	155.4	197.9	231.9	192.9	28.4	43.1	28.5
1986	160.5	218.2	260.0	210.0	27.1	44.0	28.9
1987	168.1	248.1	297.4	234.3	26.8	43.9	29.3
1988	172.3	284.1	336.7	260.7	25.7	44.1	30.2
1989	177.6	294.8	354.8	271.3	25.0	43.0	32.0
1990	190.7	304.1	363.0	281.7	27.1	41.6	31.3
1991	195.2	346.3	395.0	307.6	24.5	42.1	33.4

Annexure A.2 (*Contd.*)

Year	*Primary*	*Secondary*	*Tertiary*	*Total GDP*	*Share (%) Primary*	*Share (%) Secondary*	*Share (%) Tertiary*
1	*2*	*3*	*4*	*5*	*6*	*7*	*8*
1992	204.4	419.5	444.0	351.4	21.8	43.9	34.3
1993	214.0	502.8	491.3	398.8	19.9	47.4	32.7
1994	222.6	595.2	538.3	449.3	20.2	47.9	31.9
1995	233.7	677.7	583.4	496.5	20.5	48.8	30.7
1996	245.6	759.8	629.4	544.1	20.4	49.5	30.1
1997	254.2	839.4	687.1	592.2	19.1	50.0	30.9
1998	263.1	914.2	744.1	638.5	18.6	49.3	32.1
1999	270.5	988.6	801.6	684.1	17.6	49.4	33.0
2000	277.0	1083.7	864.1	738.8	15.9	50.9	33.2

Note.: Cols. (2) to Cols. (5) are indices, calculated at constant/comparable prices. The shares in Cols. (6) to Cols. (8) are calculated at current prices.

Source: Table 3-2, p. 50 and Table 3-4 p. 52, China Statistical Yearbook 2001, National Bureau of Statistics of China, China Statistics Press, Beijing.

Annexure A.3

Per Capita Consumption and Net Income

Year	*Income Rural*	*Income Urban*	*Consumption Rural*	*Consumption Urban*
1	*2*	*3*	*4*	*5*
1978	100.0	100.0	100.0	100.0
1979	119.2	112.7	106.1	105.2
1980	139.0	127.0	115.5	111.9
1981	160.4	127.6	125.2	123.8
1982	192.3	133.9	136.6	124.3
1983	219.6	140.6	150.8	127.4
1984	249.5	158.1	170.4	137.8
1985	268.9	160.4	194.4	147.5
1986	277.6	182.5	199.3	158.3
1987	292.0	186.9	207.9	172.0
1988	310.7	182.5	220.4	187.3
1989	305.7	182.8	218.8	184.4
1990	311.2	198.1	219.5	198.1
1991	317.4	212.4	234.2	216.6
1992	336.2	232.9	257.2	249.9
1993	346.9	255.1	272.8	272.1
1994	364.4	276.8	285.4	276.7
1995	383.7	290.3	308.7	289.6
1996	418.2	301.6	351.9	296.7
1997	437.4	311.9	363.6	307.0
1998	456.2	329.9	370.2	332.4
1999	473.5	360.6	387.6	370.1
2000	483.5	383.7	N.A.	N.A.

Note.: These are indices, calculated at constant/comparable prices.

Source: Table 3-16, p. 66 and Table 10-3 p. 304, China Statistical Yearbook 2001, National Bureau of Statistics of China, China Statistics Press, Beijing.

Annexure A.4

Investment by Source and Destination (Percentage Distribution)

I. By Destination

	State Owned Units	*Collective Owned Units*	*Individuals Economy*	*Others*
1	*2*	*3*	*4*	*5*
1981	69.48	11.98	18.54	0.00
1982	68.76	14.16	17.09	0.00
1983	66.62	10.92	22.46	0.00
1984	64.68	12.99	22.33	0.00
1985	66.09	12.86	21.05	0.00
1986	66.66	12.54	20.81	0.00
1987	64.59	14.43	20.98	0.00
1988	63.54	14.96	21.50	0.00
1989	63.67	12.93	23.40	0.00
1990	66.12	11.71	22.17	0.00
1991	66.40	12.46	21.14	0.00
1992	68.05	16.82	15.13	0.00
1993	60.64	17.73	11.29	10.34
1994	56.42	16.19	11.56	15.83
1995	54.44	16.43	12.79	16.34
1996	52.48	15.93	13.98	17.61
1997	52.49	15.44	13.75	18.32
1998	54.11	14.76	13.18	17.95
1999	53.42	14.53	14.05	18.00
2000	50.14	14.59	14.31	20.97

II. By Source

1	*State Budgetary Appropriations* *2*	*Domestic Loans* *3*	*Foreign Investment* *4*	*Fundraising and Others* *5*
1981	28.05	12.72	3.75	55.47
1982	22.70	14.32	4.88	58.10
1983	23.74	12.25	4.62	59.38
1984	22.99	14.09	3.82	59.09
1985	16.02	20.07	3.58	60.33
1986	14.59	21.10	4.39	59.92
1987	13.09	22.99	4.78	59.14
1988	9.27	21.01	5.91	63.81
1989	8.30	17.28	6.60	67.82
1990	8.70	19.60	6.29	65.41
1991	6.80	23.50	5.69	64.02
1992	4.30	27.41	5.79	62.50
1993	3.70	23.50	7.30	65.51
1994	2.97	22.42	9.92	64.69
1995	3.03	20.46	11.18	65.34
1996	2.69	19.54	11.73	66.04
1997	2.76	18.93	10.62	67.69
1998	4.17	19.30	9.11	67.42
1999	6.22	19.24	6.74	67.79
2000	6.37	20.32	5.12	68.19

Note: The shares are calculated at current prices.

Source: Table 6-2, p. 158 and Table 6-3, p. 159, China Statistical Yearbook 2001, National Bureau of Statistics of China, China-Statistics Press, Beijing.

Name Index

Subject Index